In His **TRUTH**
AND
In His **LIGHT**
A Diary of a Victim Soul

In His **TRUTH**
AND
In His **LIGHT**
A Diary of a Victim Soul

By

Linda M. Jefferson

PUBLISHING COMPANY
P.O. Box 220 • Goleta, CA 93116
(800) 647-9882 • (805) 692-0043 • Fax: (805) 967-5133

Library of Congress Number # 2002094040

Published by:
    Queenship Publishing
    P.O. Box 220
    Goleta, CA 93116
    (800) 647-9882 • (805) 692-0043 • Fax: (805) 967-5133

Printed in the United States of America

ISBN: 1-57918-219-4

TABLE OF CONTENTS

DEDICATION

I dedicate this book to God the Father, whom I love to the depths of my soul. To Jesus, whom I love for His unconditional love, forgiveness, healing and wholeness, and allowing me to suffer with Him in the Garden of Gethsemane. To the Holy Spirit whom I love for His unending knowledge of God's Holy Will, His patience, His love, and His peace. To the Blessed Mother whom I love for her patience of me and undying maternal love. To St. Therese, St. Francis, St. Padre Pio, and my Holy Guardian Angel, Mary Magdelen, for your prayerful love and guidance in helping me to suffer for God.

ACKNOWLEDGEMENT

To my husband, Jim, for his undying love and trust.

To my Mom and Dad and my sisters, Sharon and Patricia, for their unending love and support.

To Cecilia, Gabriel, Sarah, and all the unborn children in heaven for their love and prayers

To Jacqualine, Sr. Teresa Benedicta, and the Carmelite Nuns of Lafayette, and the Handmaids of the Precious Blood of New Mexico for their vigil of love, rosaries, and prayers.

To Bishop Nicholas D'Antonio, Rev. David Rabe, Msgr. Richard Carroll, Rev. Kenneth Harney, Rev. Michael McDonagh, Rev. Mossy Gallagher and Rev. John Schulte for being God's instruments in my spiritual growth with love, with compassion and with lots of patience.

To all those women and men who trusted me with their life's trials and tribulations, especially their abortion experiences.

To the suffering who have honored me with their strength and courage.

St. Joseph New American Bible. 1970
Catholic Book Publishing Co., New York

Catechism of the Catholic Church. 1992
Catholic Book Publishing Co., New York

FOREWORD

Linda Jefferson has written a story sharing her experience, strength and hope. While here in Louisiana she formed and worked with S.A.V.E. (Suffering Abortion Victims Embraced) through the Associated Catholic Charities of the Archdiocese of New Orleans. For some time I was her spiritual director. She told her story to many parish communities and became an effective minister to those who have suffered from abortions. In sharing her story she never theologized or used a model. She shared her experience and in doing so related to others in a very effective way. She has done so again by writing about her life experience as help for others.

Rev. Kenneth Harney

FOREWORD

I have known Linda Jefferson for almost two years. I remember clearly the day she introduced herself to me at the rectory. She came in sat down, looked me straight in the eye, and said, "I need to tell your some things, and I hope you will hear me out before you decide I am crazy." I found the honesty very refreshing. And that same honest, forthright approach characterizes this account of Linda's spiritual journey.

This little book is written in a very simple style. When one reads it, one feels as though he is having a conversation with Linda rather than reading some work of literature. I think that was Linda's intention. She seems absolutely uninterested in a literary career or public notoriety. Her intention is to help others to "keep going without loosing heart" as they make their way closer to the source of all true peace, God.

Linda is honest to the point of being shocking in this account, making what amounts to a public confession of sin, in the tradition of St. Augustine. And yet one does not get the impression that she is trying to shock us just for the sake of shocking us. Rather, she is trying to make clear to anyone who will read what she has written, just what marvels God can do if only His creatures allow Him.

Linda has accepted suffering from the Lord, suffering as a kind of vocation. That too, is discussed in this work. And many will find that the most difficult aspect of her life story to understand. Suffering has never been popular. In our day even otherwise good people find it almost impossible to understand how to reconcile human suffering with the existence of a loving God. Linda helps us to understand how God allows, and sometimes even inflicts suffering upon us not to do us permanent harm, but to make us more like His Son.

I have enjoyed reading this short account and hope that it will be a help to many others who are trying to become, as C. S. Lewis wrote, "creatures who can breathe the air of heaven."

Fr. John Schuete
Pastor, All Saints Church, Walton, KY
August 8, 2002 The Feast of St. Dominic

PREFACE

I am delighted to recommend to the readers of this marvelous testimonial of divine mercy and love of God the Father. Linda Jefferson shares her intimate story of sin, conversion and repentence. As Ms. Jefferson experienced the forgiveness of Jesus Christ, she was drawn to a deep personal relationship with Jesus Christ, and His Mother Mary. Her walk with Christ resulted in total surrender to the will of God the Father.

I was privileged to know Linda during a short period of this journey to the heart of the Father. On one Sunday, when I was still pastor of St. Margaret Mary church in Slidell, Linda told her story at every Mass. I have never seen so many adults weeping in my life. There was not a dry eye in church that weekend.

A little more than a year ago, I went to a conference of the "Intercessors of the Lamb," put on by Mother Nadine Brown, in Omaha, Nebraska. Unexpectedly I was asked to speak at one of the Masses. During my homily, I told Linda's story. After Mass a woman came up to me and asked if I could hear her daughter's confession. I agreed to do so, fearing that someone might be pushed into the confessional, in order to please her mother.

A 35-year-old attractive woman came in the large room for confession. "Father, my mother told you I had an abortion, I didn't have one. . .I had 7 abortions. I was living with someone at the time, who did not want children. When I became pregnant for the eighth time, I said. . .I want this child. The man was furious and we parted ways. A beautiful daughter was born to me, but every time I look at her, I see sin."

After giving this woman absolution, I prayed with this young woman. I told her how Linda Jefferson recommended naming your aborted babies. "Give each of these 7 children a name." I pleaded, "Our Lady will take them to heaven with Her."

A few months later, I received a letter form this woman, she felt she had been healed in confession. She did as I asked her and named the children. She experienced the presence of Our Blessed

Mother, with her children. . .her heart was filled with joy.

I am sure that this story could be repeated by a number of priests who have worked with Linda Jefferson. The power of her testimony unleashes the love of God the Father; true spiritual healing takes place.

This testimonial of Linda Jefferson is more than forgiveness from the effects of abortions. Linda Jefferson shares with us her painful journey to the Heart of the Father. It has resulted in becoming a victim soul. Her prayers and sufferings are valuable for the entire Church. Like Padre Pio, she suffers not for her own sins, but the sins of you and me.

I pray that this testimonial will open your heart of the love of God the Father. I hope that you understand the enormous love Linda has for Jesus and Mary. You will then discover the true meaning of love which can be found *In His Truth and In His Light*.

Rev. Msgr. Richard L. Carroll
Retired Pastor of St. Margaret Mary, Slidell

INTRODUCTION

IN HIS TRUTH AND IN HIS LIGHT is a title, I believe, that God gave to me two years ago as a prophesy for this moment in time. My personal testimony or prayer experiences are recorded in numerous journals I have kept for the past ten years by the suggestions of four Spiritual Directors. The experiences I am going to share with you in this book are real and truthful. I believe by the power of the Holy Spirit, He will gift me with the wisdom and courage to bring hope to those who need it the most. Things that are shared in this book may fill the reader with total peace, the reader may receive a better understanding as to why things happen that are out of our control. The reader may find the text either too uncomfortable or very enlightening. Sometimes the truth stings or pierces our mind, heart, and soul with understanding and wisdom, which only comes from God. We can not stand on the truth of God without standing in His light. It took me forty-four years to learn this truth and I still find that everyday is a new day in God, with God, and for God.

What I have learned the most out of all the pain and suffering I have endured is that GOD LOVES ME VERY MUCH AND HE IS IN CONTROL OF MY LIFE. Yes, I have been given a free will, but in the end, all works for the Greater Glory of God and what He believes is best for me. He is with me now and I pray that He will remain with me even unto death and after. I have also learned what saying "yes" to God really means. It means totally surrendering your entire self to Him, and depending on Him solely. God will never forsake us. In all my sinfulness, God has always been there comforting me, forgiving me, and most of all, loving me. God is pure love. It is we who forsake Him by turning our backs on Him and doing our will, which is the world, instead of His Will. A person who is truly humbly devoted to God and desires the total simplistic unity with God can journey through the threshold of God's very existence if God permits. But to experience this it takes unconditional love and trust in God whether it be in times of joy or sorrow. You must give up the world and all its attachments and surrender everything totally to God without reserve. The majority of my spiritual experiences came after I totally surrendered myself to God through the spiritual exercises of St. Ignatius of Loyola, which will be shared with you at length in Chapter 9. These spiritual experiences, which I pray will bring you hope and a new-found relationship with God, will and can be a union way beyond your comprehension. It is a relationship that two human beings are incapable of having. Why? Because human beings put stipulations on relationships. A human relationship is not pure because of the distractions of the world. God's realm is pure love. A human being's world is negative, filled with jealousy, pride, arrogance, envy, anger, unforgiveness and etc.

Many times we are asked by God to suffer for the purification of our soul or possibly to suffer to save someone else's soul. When God comes to us and asks us to suffer for Him, we respond, "Why me?" These times are usually during trials and tribulations, crises and sufferings. I have learned that suffering for God is one of the greatest gifts you can bestow upon Him, but only if you do it without a motive. You must do it with purity of heart.

The closer we grow to God through holiness and perfection, the more the evil one tries to make us trip and fall or become filled with fear, despair, or feelings of unworthiness. God is our very existence, if we allow Him to take total control of our life. We must give God total control so He can bring us through the threshold of unity with Him. He will make our heart one with His heart. How awesome!

That is where I found that Mary, Our Blessed Mother, also comes into the picture. She is a gift to us from God. A precious and wonderful gift. A gift that can be given to Roman Catholics and Non-Catholics alike. Our Blessed Mother, Mary loves everyone and will intercede to the Throne of God if only you call upon her to.

We must remember that Mary was a virgin chosen by God to conceive His Son, Jesus, by the power of the Holy Spirit, her well beloved Spouse. Mary was a single Mom and said "yes" to God out of her love and devotion to Him. God chose Joseph to be Jesus' stepfather and to take care of Mary and Jesus, which he did out of unconditional love for them and for God. Was it easy for Joseph to say "yes" to God? Not at first. God came to Joseph in a dream and revealed the truth to him which was: he was God's chosen to be the stepfather of Jesus and experience His divine conception. It was then that Joseph accepted the mission God chose for him with an acceptance out of total humility and obedience to God. How many of us say "no" to God because the mission He leads us to is not what we want for our lives. We get fearful that God will ask us to do something that may destroy our future plans. We think since we have worked so hard in our lives that we deserve all the world has to offer. But instead, we are filled with doubt, fear, anxiety or low self-worth. In the autobiography of St. Therese of Lisieux, "The Story of a Soul," written by Vernon Johnson, the book shares with us the story of the life of St. Therese and the little sacrifices that she made for God that pleased Him so much. When Therese washed the floor, she offered it up to God for His Glory. When she was reprimanded by the Mother Superior or other nuns, she lifted that up to God too. Because of the joy it brought to God's heart, He blessed her with many gifts and graces. The thing that touched me the most about St. Therese was her humanness before her death. She suffered tremendously to the point of contemplating suicide. But it was at that moment she realized that she was in the darkness and had to move to the light, where Jesus was standing.

I think of St. Padre Pio who suffered tremendously also. He had the stigmata (the five wounds of Christ). What effected me the most is how in all his suffering for the Lord he would literally drag himself to Holy Mass almost everyday just to partake in the sacrifice of Jesus. The Eucharist was extremely important to Padre Pio. Padre Pio was physically attacked by Satan many times and yet he remained focused on the Crucified Jesus. He suffered for the Holy Souls in Purgatory and even was blessed with seeing his Holy Guardian Angel, Salvatore. Millions of people would send their Guardian Angels to Padre Pio who were in desperate need of his prayers. Salvatore would send Padre Pio's message back to the person through their Holy Guardian Angel. It has been reported that Padre Pio had the gift of biolocation, which means, he could leave his body and appear to an individual who was in despair and called for his intercession. It is also reported that after his death this practice continued. Those who call upon Padre Pio for prayer say they smell roses or a unique tobacco smell of holy incense. Then I am impressed with St. Francis of Assisi who abandoned himself from his wealthy father just to embrace poverty for God in total obedience. He too received the stigmata (the five wounds of Christ). Francis would walk up to the caves to find solace and union with nature and God. He was the only saint that I am aware of that crossed the threshold of complete unity with God. Francis's heart united with Jesus' heart. They became one. Francis also suffered tremendously. In the autobiography, "Francis of Assisi—The Man Who Found Perfect Joy," by Michael De La Bedoyere, it is written, "that while on retreat on Mt. La Verna in Italy, Brother Leo witnessed Francis kneeling and singing praises to God. From heaven came a ball of light that stopped right in front of St. Francis. It was God the Father. On the same day, Francis asked God for two desires. The first was to suffer the wounds of Jesus Christ and the second desire was to love the world as Jesus did so Francis could suffer and save souls. With that prayer, an angel appeared with the Crucified Jesus and granted Francis's desires. The rays of light penetrated Francis's hands, feet and side—the five wounds of Jesus Christ were given to Francis two years before his death."

Then, in the Bible there was Rachel, a woman who lived in Ramah. Ramah was the place where Herod sent his soldiers to kill all the young boys who were age three and younger because Herod was outraged over the birth of Jesus and was trying to kill Him out of fear of Jesus becoming King. God protected the Holy Family and sent them into Egypt until Herod's death. Women who have had an abortion are compared to Rachel because of the suffering she endured over the loss of her children who were so brutally murdered.

Lastly, I am impressed with St. Mary Magdalen who lived a very promiscuous lifestyle. Not for her promiscuity, but by her total surrender of all her sinfulness to Jesus. When she heard about Jesus, she sought Him out to see what the commotion was all about on the hill of Tabor. When Jesus turned a few fish and a few pieces of bread into enough to fed thousands, that was when she began to know that she must change her heart and follow Him. While Jesus was eating with the Sanhedrin, Mary Magdalen, carrying perfumed holy oil, entered the room and knelt down before Jesus. Sorrowfully and with great humility she asked Jesus in the depths of her heart for forgiveness and began washing Jesus' feet with her tears and dried His feet with her hair. It was then her conversion began. Jesus forgave all her sins and told her to sin no more. She experienced Jesus' love, forgiveness, and mercy, just as we do in the Sacrament of Reconciliation. St. Mary Magdalen devoted herself to Jesus and stood at the foot of the cross when Jesus died and was the first person to witness His Resurrection.

You may ask, "Why is she sharing so much about the Saints with us?" It is to show you that suffering is part of living. You cannot escape it. Suffering is a purification of our soul if done in true reparation and love of Almighty God. The mentioned Saints were given to us by God as heavenly gifts to refer to, to pray to, to devote ourselves to, and to ask for their intercession to God on our behalf. But most of all, their lives ended centered in Christ, with Christ, and for Christ. At the end of our journey when God calls us home, let us hope that we can be as blessed as these Saints were by living and trusting in God so we too can spend eternity with Him in heaven.

In the next twenty chapters you will hopefully understand what living without God in your life can do to you personally and how sin can destroy your soul and very being. Conversion and transformation with God brings new life, a life that is joyful and wonderful in good times and in bad times. GOD LOVES YOU AND I SO MUCH THAT HE SENT HIS ONLY SON, JESUS, TO DIE FOR OUR SINS. What father would do that? Only God.

In this book, it is our hope that some experiences will bring you peace, and show you the importance of living in the truth and light of God, not in the world of oppression, despair and darkness. My own experiences have been very difficult for me. Even writing this book, which I believe with all my heart is God's Will, it is still difficult for me to share my whole entire life with you and confront issues that are so private. When I took this to prayer, the Holy Spirit softly and gently reassured me that I was to constantly empty my-self so He could speak the words that God wants shared and writ-ten. God does not want fear, pride, or arrogance to enter. I do this for the love and glory of God the Father with whom I belong too; body, mind, soul, and spirit. I could not have written this book without the support of my family also.

The experiences I will speak about are abortion, miscarriage and hysterectomy, which led to the beginning of my conversion, molestation and masturbation, the break up of my family at age eighteen, my twenty year old marriage and being a stepmother of five, our move to Louisiana, which attributed to my second conver-sion, totally surrendering and moving to Kentucky to continue God's Will, the deeply spiritual journey with God that has brought me to the understanding of the joy of suffering for God, and finally, cross-ing the threshold to God through the Triumph of the Immaculate Heart of Mary. This journey has been so miraculous that only God could have been the artist of it all. Praise Be to God!

Linda M. Jefferson

1

IN THE BEGINNING

I was born in a small town called Mine Hill, New Jersey. The population was approximately 2,000 people. There was a corner store called "Josie's," and a small bank. Life in Mine Hill was good. My older sister, Patricia, had her friends and I had mine. We were like night and day. Everyone in the neighborhood would refer to me as Shirley Temple because of my natural curly hair, big blue eyes and how Mom would dress me in the cutest dresses. The neighbors would invite me into their homes and give me milk and cookies. I always seemed to get all the attention. At age three, my little sister, Sharon, was born. Then things changed. Today, professionals have titled this syndrome; "middle child syndrome." Middle child syndrome is when the middle child feels left out and unloved from both parents. The middle child will try to excel in everything they take part in or they become rebellious to seek attention. For the first three years of my life, I was the big cheese, until Sharon came along, then resentment set in. Mom and Dad would always try to involve me in playing with Sharon, changing her diapers and feeding her, but who cared about those icky dirty diapers, not me, I just wanted to play and have fun the way it used to be without a baby sister who took all the attention away from me. So I began doing things to get attention. As I remember when I turned four Mom and Dad bought me a sandbox. It was beautiful and had a canopy top. I would have fun for hours. Now I was very protective of this sandbox and was very selective with whom I would allow into it. Frankie, the little boy I played with, would try to come on my side, so I would take my little plastic shovel and draw a line down the center of the sandbox to let Frankie know that he could not go beyond the line I made. If he did, he was in trouble. Well. Frankie had to test me, so I grabbed his arm and bit him. He ran home crying. Frankie did not learn his lesson the first time, so I bit him again. After the third time of my bite marks on poor little Frankie's arm, Frankie's Mom brought him over to show Mom what I had done. I remember his Mom saying, "Lois, something needs to be done about this." Of course, Mom agreed. I remember running into the house to hide. Well, of course, my mother found me and took me outside. She grabbed my little arm and stuck it in Frankie's face and said to him, "Bite her." Well, Frankie did not hold back. He bit me so hard that it broke the skin of my little precious arm and I was bleeding. I ran into the house screaming as if someone had just torn off my arm. I turned to Mom for sympathy and she said, "I am sorry I had to do this sweetie, but you have to stop biting that poor little boy and I thought if you felt the pain Frankie was going through, it would cause you to stop." Believe me I understood exactly what Mom was saying. From that time forward I never bit Frankie or anyone else again. Lesson learned.

Still, at this young age, confusion set in about how an adult neighbor treated me when he would invite me into his home regularly for milk and cookies. I will share the entire story with you in the next chapter.

Another childhood experience I remember so clearly was a game that my friend, Kathy, and I would play. It was a crazy game we both made up. It reminded me of hide-and-seek. It would make us laugh. One of us would ride Kathy's bike to the end of the driveway while the other would hide somewhere in the garage. Since we took turns, it was my turn to hide in the garage. Fearless Linda climbed anywhere so I would not be found. Since all the good places were already used, I decided to climb up on the picnic table that had four folding chairs piled on top of it. I climbed up into the chairs and sat down. Under the picnic table was a pipe with a sharp point on it. The chairs tipped over and I fell and hit the back of my head on the pipe. Kathy screamed and her Mom came running. All I remember was that Mom came running and then I passed out. When I awoke, I found myself in a hospital bed, in the hospital. Mom and Dad were crying at the bedside, but I did not know who they were. I had amnesia. I vaguely remember a nurse coming into my room to prick my finger to take blood. I screamed at the top of my lungs because it hurt so bad. For one week I was unconscious and my brain was swelling. To relieve the pressure in my head, the doctor had decided to drill a hole into the top of my skull. As they

In the beginning

were getting ready to wheel me down to surgery, I awoke and recognized Mom and Dad, who were so happy. God really does work in miraculous ways. I believe God answered everyone's prayers and spared us anymore suffering. After I recovered from the ordeal, it seemed it was time to get ready to start kindergarten, which I was really looking forward too. I enjoyed being creative with finger paints by making a real mess or drawing happy things. Just like most mothers, Mom seemed so impressed with her child's creativity and would hang the drawings on the refrigerator for everyone to see. It really gave us kids a sense of accomplishment, acceptance, and a healthy self-image.

When it was time to start first grade, I really had a difficult time leaving Mom because fun time was over. I would cry every morning before we left for school and I would beg Mom to let me stay home with her and Sharon. The thought of leaving them was devastating for me. But Mom was the strong one. She knelt down, hugged me, loved all over me, and encouraged me to go to school and learn everything I could because it was so important. An hour later she would have to come back to the school because the Principal would call her to inform her I was disturbing the class with my crying. Finally, the Principal asked why I was so unhappy. Out of my mouth came that my best friend found a new friend and they did not want to play with me. I was crushed beyond words. The Principal called both girls into his office with me sitting there. He spoke to us about playing together. After his talk, we all played together and the crying ended. I loved school after that.

As Sharon grew older, we became closer. On weekends and after school we would play with our Barbie, Ken and Midge dolls under the cherry tree in our front yard. We really enjoyed each others company. She looked up to me for everything. It was a neat feeling. Sharon was included in playing with my friends. We played hide-and-seek, caught lightning bugs, and pretended to be singers as we sang and danced in the middle of the street for everyone to see. We all loved the attention that the adults gave us, especially when the Good Humor ice cream truck came on the street. Our parents would buy us ice cream. It was so good.

As school progressed, the teachers realized that I had a learn-

3

ing disability, especially with reading and comprehension. The school put me in a special class, which I did well. After a period of time I could read well. Some kids in school made fun of the children who were in the special class. We read slow, which upset some of the class, but we ignored their attacks.

When I was nine years old I was being prepared for Holy Communion at Sunday School. My teacher was a Dominican Nun by the name of Sister Victoria. I loved Sister Victoria. She took me under her wing and helped me to get prepared for the special day. One Sunday as we were walking to the school after Mass, the wind was blowing quite hard and I was awestruck watching the nuns habits flow in the breeze. Their rosaries were clinging as they walked to the school. They looked like they were angels gliding and almost flying in the wind. It was wonderful to see nuns in long habits.

Today, Our Holy Father, Pope John Paul II, has called all of the religious order of nuns back to their habits. I always believed if a woman is called to be a nun, then she should dress like one. It brings respect and imitates Our Blessed Mother. Today, most orders dress in regular street clothes and wear make-up and jewelry. I have often prayed in sadness for them. I believe that it is one of the reasons that religious orders are not growing because the traditional beliefs have almost disappeared. Liberalization and the world has touched the very purpose of convents all over the world. What joy it would bring if nuns would return to their habits and traditional beliefs so women would answer the call to serve God as His beloved daughters. If a person would see a religious nun today, the question would be, "What is missing from this nun?" I thank God for Sister Victoria, the beautiful nun who touched my life, because I knew I was being called to become a nun. Spiritually, Sister Victoria was preparing me for the convent by allowing herself to be used by God as His instrument in bringing me to Him as His bride. I accepted the calling joyfully, even though I did not share this calling with my family because Sister Victoria and I decided to wait until my high school graduation night. But something devastating happened that would alter my life forever. I will share this with you in depth in chapter three. Even though I was rebellious at times, the rest of my childhood seemed normal. In high school, especially my junior and senior year, I befriended a group of teens who were into Janice Joplin, a singer who was a big name in the sixties and seventies and who died of an overdose of drugs. I found myself fixing my hair and dressing just like Janice. Then I was introduced to marijuana and other drugs by individuals who you would have thought were so straight. My parents never knew about the drugs because I was on the honor roll and on the high school drill team and they were focused on their failing marriage. Plus, I was very good at hiding things from them and escaping from family pain.

I had a party at my house one Friday night. My parents were home supervising the party so alcohol and drugs were not acceptable, nor were they allowed into our home. Some of the boys would sit and talk to Mom, while Dad would patrol the outside to make sure the kids were behaving themselves. Mom was always impressed with the behavior of the young teens at the party because they were respectful of my parents and our home. Some of the boys stayed after the party to help Mom and I clean up. Now Mom was really impressed. Since everyone had so much fun, they decided to spread a rumor around school that I was having another party the following Friday night, which did not go over well with my parents, especially when the cars started pulling up in front of the house. Dad went out, nixed the party, and sent everyone home. Mom wanted me to date this one boy who told her I would not date him. He was a very nice guy—a jock—but I had my eyes on someone else, who of course would not give me the time of day, which did not hurt my feelings at all. At age eighteen, I remained a virgin because I knew in my heart my true calling. Guys were not in God's plan for me.

In the junior and senior year of high school, I took beauty culture to become a beautician. I laughed to myself at the thought of a nun who was a beautician. Part of the class was learning how to do theatrical make-up. I became so engrossed in what I was learning. The teacher showed us how to age someone from a child to an elderly person. The stages were phenomenal. Then she taught us how to do injuries, the blood and guts kind of stuff. Our school would have theatrical plays every year, so our class was asked to do the make-up. I was so excited. I knew I had a talent and so did the teacher. I found hair styling very boring. When the lead actor of the play asked me to personally do his make-up, I was shocked. The teacher was very supportive. The lead actor, Gary, happened to be my first love when we were in fourth grade. Gary's role in the play went from a young man to an elderly man. I was fascinated by it. Next thing I knew other cast members requested me to do their make-up too. It gave me self-worth. I finally found something that I could excel in. It was an escape for me into a world of false joy, of temptation, and of a lure away from God.

Today, I look back and see that I really did not have the calling to be a beautician or to do theatrical make-up. I was called to be the bride of God, even though at the time I found myself excelling more and more into the theatrical world. But the calling to be a nun never left my mind and heart. Friends could not understand why I did not pursue a theatrical career because of my talent as a make-up artist. No one knew the struggle and torment I was having. I kept hearing the voice of God say, "How long must I wait for you?" It was then that my whole world turned upside down and I found solace inside myself because my family was being torn apart and anger was setting in.

2

MOLESTATION AND MASTURBATION

As I began to share with you in Chapter 1, at age three I would go to our neighbor's house for milk and cookies. One day Mom came home from work and my father, my sisters and I were down in the basement watching television. We hugged Mom to welcome her home and then I turned to her and said, "Mom look what I learned today!" I was lying on the couch masturbating or rocking myself back and forth with my hands together in a fist at my private area. The sensation felt good. Mom and Dad were horrified and wanted to know where I learned it from. Not remembering, I told them I saw it on television. Mom spanked me and sent me to my room. Sharing a room and double bed with my sister, Patricia, I would rock myself in my sleep. Of course, this would wake Patricia up from a sound sleep and she would get Mom. My parents were beside themselves. They did not know where to turn. They took me to a doctor who told them I would grow out of the action, which of course, did not bring comfort to my parents. The act continued and I could not control myself.

This went on until I was eighteen years of age. I finally spoke to a priest who was sent by God. He was truthful about the ramification of the actions. His counseling helped me to break the habit, even though I knew in my heart that it was God who saved me from this degrading act. I always kept in my heart how I wanted to please God, not offend Him, even though I failed miserably.

I could not understand why as a child I could not sit on Dad's lap or any other man's lap, but yet I could do this horrendous act. Throughout my life I could never see a face in my nightmares and often asked Mom if she knew who the faceless man could be who was doing bad things to me. Mom would always say, "No," and I knew to the depths of my soul she was speaking the truth.

When Dad found out about the nightmares, he would cry because he did not know how to help me. It was sad that the relationship between Dad and I became strained because I could not trust men, even Dad whom I loved so much and he loved me. I believed every man was trying to hurt me. The flashbacks and nightmares continued with always a faceless man. As years went on I tried to bury the entire situation because it was too painful.

On Mother's Day, May 1993, we rushed Mom to the hospital. She was bleeding internally, passed out onto the floor, and was making gargling sounds when she breathed. The toilet was full of blood. We called 911 and proceeded to the emergency room. After pumping out four pints of blood from her stomach, it was discovered that she had a bleeding peptic ulcer that was ready to perforate. Mom was suffocating in her blood and she was dying. Mom asked Jim to accompany her to the room, while Sharon and I stayed in the waiting room crying and praying, not knowing if Mom was going to live or die. We entrusted Mom to the Immaculate Heart of Mary for her intercession.

The nurse in the emergency room told us that if we would have waited until morning to bring her to the hospital, Mom would have been dead. I believe Our Blessed Mother was with Mom because of Mom's deep love and devotion to Our Blessed Lady.

When we called our sister, Patricia, she flew by plane from New Jersey to Louisiana to be with Mom. The doctor told us Mom was in serious condition and he would like us to take shifts to be with her for the next forty-eight hours. Trying to leave our faith in God and the Blessed Mother, we took shifts. Since Patricia is a nurse, she wanted to stay with Mom until she was out of danger.

When Jim, Sharon and I arrived the next morning at the hospital, we were joking about my birth and when I was little. I made a comment to Mom and Patricia that I was probably adopted or the neighbor's daughter because I was born with bright red hair. No one laughed or felt the comment was funny. Patricia had this serious look on her face. Then Patricia looked at me and said, "You do not remember, do you?" Dismayed, I replied, "Remember what?" Hesitatingly Patricia proceeded to tell me how this neighbor molested me at age three, the same time I had learned to masturbate. Even though the neighbor never penetrated me, he did rock me on his hardened private part. Patricia and I could see Mom was getting upset. She asked Patricia where she was when all this was happening. My sister said, "Don't you remember when I would run to you when he would come over our house because he would always kiss me on the mouth with his mustache that was like a brillo pad, or I would run up to my room?"

Mom began to cry. The conversation ended because the doctor told us to make sure Mom did not get upset. Patricia, Sharon, and I decided to go out for dinner that night. Patricia shared with me what she had witnessed the neighbor doing to me. She was seven years old and afraid to say anything. A rage grew up inside of me and all I could think about was the years lost with my Dad. All I kept saying to myself was, "Why God, why did she let me go through this?" After Mom had recovered and Patricia went home, the rage began to turn to hatred for the neighbor and Patricia. It had gotten to the point that I would not allow my husband to touch me. I blamed the neighbor and Patricia for the entire thing.

I knew I had to do something about the rage and hatred I was experiencing because I was ready to explode, so I decided to go to confession. God blessed me with Father Mossy Gallagher, who is the most humble, gentle, and kind man. When I entered the confessional, I sat down in front of Father Mossy and began to tell him the entire story. I was hysterical and Father Mossy was crying also. Once he calmed down and then calmed me down, he told me to go into the Eucharistic Adoration Chapel and scream at God for not interceding for me, and then forgive Patricia and the neighbor. "Put the man in God's hands," Father Mossy said.

I went into the Eucharistic Adoration Chapel which was empty. I thought I was losing my mind, but I did not care. I believed Father Mossy knew what he was talking about. The screaming went on for a short time until I got the anger and hatred out of my system. Finally, I knelt down in the front pew closest to Jesus on the Cross. Crying profusely, I felt the True Presence of the Lord before me. I entrusted the neighbor, who is now dead, to the Lord and begged the Lord to forgive him. Then I begged God to forgive me for screaming at Him. I began to pray for the man and an enormous peace entered my heart and I knew that the Lord accepted my request and my forgiveness of the neighbor and Patricia. I felt Jesus hold me in His loving arms and comforting me. It felt wonderful. I was overwhelmed with His love and peace and the Lord removed all the hurt and pain from my mind and heart. I realized then how frightened Patricia really was and it was not her fault for what had happened.

The healing began and I could now put the experience behind me and begin to move on in God's love and peace. Today, I come in contact with many individuals who have had a similar experience, if not the same as mine. I speak about my experience and always Praise God for Father Mossy who was God's chosen instrument to help me find peace and to let go of the entire experience. Father Mossy has confirmed to me how powerful the Sacrament of Reconciliation really is. Father Mossy is a holy, humble, obedient, and loving servant of God. I will never forget this priest who represents Jesus Christ. He comforted me and cried with me in my time of despair and desolation. Father Mossy is a true shepherd of God. I will forever Praise God for the gift and grace that He bestowed upon me with this humble priest.

3

THE BREAK-UP OF A FAMILY

When I turned seventeen years of age, I noticed that my parents were having marital problems. The family did not attend Mass anymore, which upset me deeply because of the calling I had to be a nun. On my eighteenth birthday, I had planned to tell my parents of the calling to religious life. The arguing and bickering was more than my sisters and I could stand. I turned to God, but found no solace. I prayed and prayed for our family to stay together, but we all seemed to be drifting further and further apart. My heart went out to my baby sister, Sharon, who was only fourteen at the time.

People in the neighborhood were verbally attacking Mom, calling her all kinds of names. She was so devastated and depressed when she heard the word "divorce." I kept pleading with God not to let our family break up. But still I found no solace. I spoke to a priest who told me it was not my fault or the fault of my sisters. It was between Mom and Dad. Financial problems arose and we had to put our home up for sale. Dad was unable to work due to back surgery. I begged Mom to do something to prevent this from taking place, but all she could do was cry. She went to a therapist who prescribed tranquilizers for her depression. The more my parents fought, the more I began to stay out of the house all hours of the night. Graduation from high school was approaching quickly. The calling to religious life was beginning to become only a dream. I began to get angry at God for not interceding. I turned to drugs and alcohol to numb my pain. I was hardly home and I would stay over a friend's house for peace and fun.

Working part-time in a department store, I met a young man by the name of Doug who was twenty-four years old. I thought he was the coolest guy I had ever met. I invited Doug to my high school graduation, which displeased my parents since they disliked him. The rage inside of me over the divorce caused me to ignore and not respect my parents feelings and so I began to date Doug. On my eighteenth birthday, still being a virgin, I gave into the passion of Doug. I loved everything about him. It was my escape from what was taking place at home.

The divorce was finalized and Mom and Sharon, who were devastated over the divorce more than I, decided to go on a vacation for two weeks. When Mom asked where I was going to stay, I lied to her and told her I was staying with a friend. When they left for their vacation, I moved in with Doug. Now living in mortal sin and with the rage of the divorce continuing to grow deeper, I tossed all the plans of religious life away. All that mattered to me was Doug. I stopped taking drugs and lived a life of justified happiness. Doug and I would have lengthy conversations about getting married and starting a family, but in the depths of my heart I knew something was not right. I got a full-time job at a telephone company not far from where we lived. Then things began to happen between Doug and I that was beyond repair. That story will continue in chapter four.

When Mom and Sharon returned from vacation, they were devastated that I deliberately moved in with Doug. I decided to live with the very man no one in my family could accept. Mom was kind to Doug, but hurt because of what I had done. She told me that she was going to rent an apartment for a while, but she really wanted to move to Florida. Our family had totally drifted apart. Things between Doug and I ended and I moved into the apartment with Mom and Sharon temporarily. In one month they were moving to Florida and I had to decide what to do. Dad and Patricia had an apartment together and told me they would make room for me to live with them. I told them I would think about it.

On the very day Mom and Sharon were leaving for Florida, I called Mom and told her I quit my job and I was moving to Florida with them. Driving 70 miles an hour in a 45 mile an hour zone, I was pulled over and given a speeding ticket. I gave the ticket and money to Patricia, sold my car to a neighbor, and the three of us left for our new home in Florida. As we were driving, Mom asked me why I changed my mind to go with them. I shared with them that on my way to work that morning, I heard a loud voice in my heart say, "Move to Florida with your mother and your sister because they will need you." They were shocked, but happy I listened to the voice. They told me that they were both hoping and praying I would have a change of heart.

Life in Florida was not an easy one at first. We were running out of money and I had a difficult time finding a job. This went on for months. When we were down to our last penny, I got a job in a hospital. Mom found a new home to purchase using her Veterans benefits and we moved into it. The house was so nice. Sharon was ready to graduate from high school. I was saving lots of money, while helping Mom financially. Financially things were beginning to improve, so I decided to purchase a new Ford Mustang because I needed a car to go to work and instead of taking the bus.

I befriended a young lady at the hospital who I would hang out with during my free time and days off. She had her own apartment. Having my own apartment was a dream of mine because Sharon and I were not getting along. One day she made me so angry that I pinned her into a corner of the kitchen and put a knife to her throat. I knew then it was time for me to leave. The rage I had buried was surfacing and I was taking it out on Mom and Sharon. I moved in with my friend, which lasted only three months. I quit my job at the hospital and moved back in with Mom and Sharon. I was beginning to feel out of control inside. I was so afraid I was going to hurt someone. I got another job and was making even more money.

I became obsessed with the world and materialism. It meant everything to me. When I heard the voice of God in the pit of my heart, I would reject Him and bury His words. Only rage and hatred would swell up inside of me. I felt so alone, but refused to go to confession where I always found solace. I wanted to be held by God so desperately, just like in the past. He made the pain go away, but of course, I was too proud. In the darkness of the night while lying in bed unable to sleep, I would hear God speaking to my heart. His voice was becoming so loud that I found it difficult to block Him out. I hated myself and I could not live with myself any longer. I moved out of Mom's house again to be alone. The loneliness was unbearable. Thoughts of suicide rang in my mind. I believed it was the only answer for the hurt and pain I caused my family. What led me to this state? In the next chapter you will hopefully understand why my behavior was the way it was. I could not justify or make excuses for my behavior any longer. It was time to confront the demons, be healed and find God. God's truth and light of my life was surfacing and I could not accept what I was seeing.

4

CHOOSING DEATH OVER LIFE

This chapter is a continuance of my relationship with Doug, the coolest man I ever met and the man I loved so much. When I moved in with Doug, I turned my back on the one person who loved me the most, God. Of course, I did not see it that way at the time. I just saw anger and rage.

In the last chapter I shared with you that Doug and I spoke of marriage and a family. One night Doug wanted to have sex and I told him I thought I could get pregnant. He very innocently and pridefully said he would pull out in time and I had nothing to worry about. Since I trusted this man, we had intercourse. Four weeks later, no menstrual period. Eight weeks later, no menstrual period. A little voice inside said, "You are pregnant."

I went to the doctor and he confirmed the pregnancy. I was so happy to be carrying our child that I came home from the doctor ecstatic. I told Doug I had something wonderful to tell him. "Surprise honey! We are going to have a baby!" I said. He collapsed in his chair with this very somber look on his face and told me to sit down. When I sat down, still so joyful at the news of a baby, Doug was not. In fact, he was upset.

He preceded to explain that now was not the time for a child and that we had to have an abortion. When I asked what an abortion was, he explained the procedure to me. The only words I heard were you are no longer going to be pregnant. I was horrified. Our dream, I thought, was coming true and now he did not want to have our baby who I believed was conceived out of love.

For days I was crying. There was silence between Doug and I. Then one morning he called me at work and told me we were going to New York. When I asked why, he just informed me that a clinic there performs abortions. I began begging him not to put me through the procedure. I cried and argued until I could not any longer.

I felt so alone. I could not go to my parents because they were having their own problems. I had no where to turn. Doug was adamant about ending the life of our child and did not care about my feelings. He promised me we would still get married and have children, but now was not the time. Weak and beaten down with no where to turn or no where to go, the appointment was made.

It was a cold and dreary day in winter and the cold temperature remained inside the car on the way to New York. I kept crying and begging Doug to change his mind, but it did not matter because his mind was made up.

When we arrived at the abortion clinic, an assistant asked us to fill out paperwork and pay cash for the procedure. Then Doug and I followed the assistant into a room where four other couples were waiting. She began to explain what was going to take place. She told us that our eight week old babies were nothing but blobs of tissue, pieces of nothings, the "procedure" was legal, painless, and safe. She also told us that in a matter of minutes the procedure would be over and we could go with our lives. I cried uncontrollably, which irritated and embarrassed Doug. I was the last one to be called to go into the room where this so called "procedure" was to take place. Before entering the room, I turned to Doug and begged him not to put me through it. His response was, "If you love me, Linda, you will do this for me."

Feeling dejected, I entered the room. In the room were two nurses who were waiting my arrival. I removed my clothes and one of the nurses gave me a needle with a pain killer in it, and injected me in my bottom half. The abortionist entered the room, but never made eye contact with me. Two other nurses stood on each side of the table. The abortionist told me I would feel some discomfort. The pain was excruciating. I began to scream. Then he turned on what sounded like a high powered vacuum cleaner and began sucking out what felt like was my organs. I sat up and told him to stop and he could only reply it was too late. All of a sudden the four nurses fell down on top of me so the abortionist could finish his job. All I remember was screaming "STOP," but it was too late. The so called "procedure" was over.

The abortionist and nurses left the room and one of the nurses came back into the room with a tampon because I was bleeding.

She also gave me medication to take for a week or two. All I could do was cry. The nurse told me to snap out of it and she was going to take me to recovery. I laid in recovery with four other women, all like me, crying uncontrollably. "What did I do?" I asked myself. The pain was unbearable. I felt like I was dying. I had to get out of there. I put my clothes on and proceeded to the waiting room where Doug was sitting. He spotted me and said, "How do you feel, honey?" With that, I vomited all over him. After he was able to clean up, we started to drive back home to New Jersey. Doug purchased a new Ford Mustang, which we drove to New York. On the way home I vomited all over his new car. I could not stop vomiting. I was so ill. I went to bed as soon as we returned to the apartment.

Our relationship changed dramatically. I was angry, mostly at myself, but also with him for this traumatic experience that took place. I hated to be around him. I continued to cry and cry. Then he told me he thought it would be best if I moved out and moved in with Mom and Sharon because he joined the army. At first I was devastated, but my anger for him helped me to accept it. Once I moved in with Mom, I found out through friends that Doug was dating my best girlfriend, anyway I thought she was my best girlfriend. WRONG!!!! The relationship with Doug was over. He went his way and I went mine.

As I shared in the previous chapter, Mom, Sharon, and I moved to Florida. While I was living on my own, I met new friends. One night we took drugs and drank alcohol and went to party at a Disco Bar. A young man by the name of Gary asked me to dance. That was all I remembered. The next morning I woke up in his bed with no clothes on. A little voice inside of me said, "You are pregnant." When I went to the doctor eight weeks later, he confirmed the pregnancy. I was shocked. My girlfriend sat me down and told me because of my addiction to drugs and alcohol it would be better to have an abortion.

Convinced she was right and being in a total state of denial over the first abortion, I went through with the second abortion. My girlfriend took me to the abortion clinic where I was told the exact same things as the first time. Gary told me he fell out of a tree when he was young and he was sterile, so the baby was not his. I became cold-hearted, numb, angry and hateful. Life did not matter to me anymore. I was a zombie. My lifestyle was sex, drugs, and alcohol.

My girlfriend told me to stay with her that night. During the night, I came down with a fever, infection set in, and I began to hemorrhage. She rushed me to the hospital where I was told that the abortionist was in a hurry and tore my womb, and I needed a hysterectomy. I looked at the doctor as if he was crazy. He gave me medication for the infection and referred me to a gynecologist. After seeing three gynecologists, all confirming the inevitable, a hysterectomy. I was horrified at the thought of never having children again. I began escaping inside myself and running the streets. Like I said, my life was sex, drugs, and alcohol. Life meant nothing to me anymore.

Finally, I met this really nice Roman Catholic man whom I dated off and on. From the moment I met him I knew one day we were going to get married. I got off the drugs entirely, but still drank alcohol. One night in a heat of passion, we had sex once and I swore it would not happen again. In fact, our relationship ended. Six weeks later I woke up in excruciating pain. I was hemorrhaging clots of blood. I called my girlfriend, who lived thirty minutes away from me. She came to take me to the hospital. While waiting for her, I was sitting on the toilet to relieve some of the pain. When I looked into the toilet all I could see was blood. When we arrived at the hospital, the doctor examined me. He asked me if I was pregnant and I told the doctor that I did not think so. He said he did not see any signs of pregnancy, but to him it sounded like I may have miscarried. Three children gone now and still I refused to accept it. I was good in burying things. I did it all my life, so what would have stopped me from continuing this pity party of denial?

One week later I had the hysterectomy. When people would ask me why I had to have a hysterectomy, I would lie and say it was because I was pre-cancerous. Recuperation time from surgery was six weeks and I stayed in my apartment very depressed and suicidal. I attempted suicide twice from an overdose. I just could not live with myself any longer. Finally, I got down on my knees and begged God to help me. I knew I was searching for love in all the wrong places. I needed a man in my life who would love me unconditionally and give me stability. I believe God answered that prayer by sending back to me the Roman Catholic man, Jim. He was divorced twice with five children. The two youngest children were the same age and sex as the babies I aborted.

I knew Jim was sent by God from the moment we met and I never doubted that. It saddens me that it took all this suffering, pain, and sinfulness to get me to turn my focus back to God. I thank God He did not turn away from me. He was with me during this painful time, comforting me, and loving me unconditionally.

We, as human beings, think we have all the answers to life. For the most part we believe that we must be in total control of our lives, especially our bodies and that no one is going to tell us, as women, what to do with our bodies. But in God's realm, which should be our realm too, our bodies belong to God, not us. Our bodies should be a temple of the Holy Spirit, free from sin and impurities. Life to God is the most precious gift He can bestow upon us. But yet, we destroy life by becoming a disposable society. We have lost our focus and direction as a world who allows the killing of innocent unborn children and allows our elderly to be euthanized. Something is wrong with this picture. Life is a beautiful gift from God from conception to natural death. Let us refocus our lives and give back the control of our lives to a God who only wants what is best for us by loving us unconditionally. GOD WILL NEVER FORSAKE US BECAUSE HE LOVES US SO MUCH NEVER TO LEAVE US WHERE WE ARE.

Through these experiences I learned to take responsibility for my actions. It was a responsibility I ran from all my life. These actions are not something I am proud of. In fact, I was ashamed for what I had done. An abortion experience is a trauma that can be forgiven, but can never be forgotten. Whenever I counseled someone or spoke publicly, I relived the abortion experience over and over.

I believe, that through God's love, forgiveness, and mercy, He has called me forth to help those who are suffering like I did. Then they can also experience God's love, healing, and wholeness. As long as I live on this earth, I will serve God to the best of my ability In His Truth and In His Light, and I will be the smallest instrument possible in saving His children from suffering from the trauma of abortion by bringing them back to Him.

5

MARRIAGE AND STEPMOTHERHOOD

Jim and I were married in a Methodist Church on July 4, 1981. Since Jim was married twice before me, we went through the annulment process of the Roman Catholic Church with Father Michael McDonagh. On November 23, 1982, our annulment was approved by the Tribunal of the Diocese of St. Petersburg, Florida. On December 19, 1982, Father McDonagh married us at Holy Cross Church.

Jim and I had many problems to work out for the first couple of years of our marriage. Being put in the role of stepmother to five beautiful children was a bit overwhelming, since Jim's youngest children were the same ages as my aborted children, Cecilia and Gabriel.

Jim's youngest daughter was the flower girl in our wedding and his youngest son was too small to attend. The children were leery of me at first, but his daughter and I made friends quickly. His son and I loved one another instantly until his mother caused complications and division in the relationship.

Father McDonagh was helping me through the turmoil that was affecting me emotionally, psychologically and spiritually. The bottom line was, I needed alot of healing. I knew Father McDonagh was a vessel sent by God to me because in our meetings he was so opened to the power of God's Holy Spirit. A truly gifted man and priest to this day.

He would say things to me that only God knew. That is how focused Father McDonagh was. One session he had me close my eyes and focus on Jesus standing before me. Then Father McDonagh told me to look in Jesus' eyes and experience the love He has for me. I did what was requested and the experience was beyond my comprehension. Then Father McDonaugh told me to allow Jesus to embrace me, which I did. The unconditional love and peace was beyond the love and peace of humanity. It is difficult to express the love of the Lord.

Father McDonagh met with me regularly and helped me to experience a total healing of my heart, my mind, my body, and my soul. It was then that a second conversion took place. For the first time in my life, I could honestly say that I loved God again with my whole being. Father McDonagh was transferred after Jim and I went through the Life in the Spirit Seminar given at the Church. Father McDonagh gave us a prophetic word, "Be very careful of those who claim to be gifted and are not. It is those who you must stay away from or you could become lost." Those words rang out in my heart and Jim and I took them seriously because we witnessed for ourselves exactly what Father McDonagh was talking about. Two women who proclaimed to be prophetic tried to break our marriage up. Of course, this made me more aware of how evil can infiltrate even the Charismatic Movement.

Jim and I went on our first Marriage Encounter Weekend. Jim and I argued all the way over to the hotel where they were holding the weekend because that was Jim's golf weekend. But I knew that God wanted us there so we could learn how to communicate with each other.

The weekend was grueling. If you have never been on a Marriage Encounter Weekend, I recommend it highly, especially if there are problems in your marriage. Jim and I laughed, cried, and got to know one another on a deep loving and respectful level. The hardest subject was death. It was then we totally surrendered to God and made a lifetime commitment to one another. God lifted the pain and suffering we were both feeling. He filled our hearts with an overabundance of love, and brought us closer than we had ever been before in our marriage.

Those individuals who are reading this and are the stepparent, it is not easy. Since I was from a broken home, I can relate with the children who have a very difficult time accepting a stranger into their lives. I know at age forty-six, I still believe in my heart that my parents should never have been divorced and I will go to my grave believing it. This is not to say my stepmother is a horrible person, because she is not. I just believe that marriage is forever and that once God brings two people He has chosen together to become one with Him, let no man bring them asunder, which means, let no man or woman destroy or divide what God has brought together.

Mom never married again. She felt there was only one true love in her life and that was Dad. She has sacrificed her life for her three girls. I thank God every day for blessing me with Mom. She is the type of woman that everyone loves. She has emotionally adopted hundreds of children over the years. It has been incredible.

Before Jim and I ever took our vows, I believed that his children would love me and I would love them. I also believed that everything would run smoothly. Boy was I wrong. The children just wanted their parents back together. The children did not accept the fact that their Dad had someone else in his life. It was difficult for everyone.

Jim and I decided to join a Marriage Encounter Circle Meeting with people we befriended from Church. There were six couples including ourselves. We met once a month at a different couple's home. Our circle was a breath of fresh air because we could identify with each other and so well that we clicked so wonderfully. God was definitely the center of our circle, our marriages, and our own lives. The monthly meetings gave us time to vent. It was wonderful. Then during the month each couple would continue dialoguing with their spouses in the privacy of their own homes. The couple would pick the topic and write their feelings and emotions in a notebook. Sometimes it would just be love letters to each other. Sometimes we were not afforded the time needed because of family problems. I know without any doubt in my mind and heart that without the continuation of Marriage Encounter, Jim and I would be divorced because of the enormous pressure and stress we were under.

I tried so hard to be a good stepmother, but more times than others, I would fall flat on my face. The youngest daughter could not handle living with her mother and asked to come and live with her Dad and I. We agreed. That was when she realized that I was not the bad person she was told I was. She stayed for one year, then decided to go back home because Jim and I were too strict. We saw both children every other weekend when they lived close to us.

Their mother decided to move to another state with them. They would come once a year to visit, mainly during the summer when they were out of school or Christmas time. The children missed their Dad desperately, so their mother moved them back to Florida.

Jealously of the ex-spouses always seemed to get in the way of rearing the children in a positive way. If divorced parents could only get along for the sake of the children, this world would be a better place. But there are those jealous divorced parents who just want to make the other parent's new life a living hell. This reflects on the behavior patterns of the children. The children do not do well in school because of the emotional roller coaster they feel they are on. The children can also be used as a pawn between the divorced parents. All professionals would tell us that this is the worse abuse you can do to a child.

When a child is being used, they seem to turn on the other parent out of simple confusion. Then of course the stepparent is considered the evil person for breaking up the family, which nine times out of ten is not true.

Today, single parent families are on the rise. I know when my family broke up, I turned to drugs and alcohol to try and to escape from all the madness of divorce. Today, we find our children acting out their anger, hatred, confusion and pain on others. We have children being killed in our schools, in our streets, and in our homes.

The value of life is being snuffed out by the forces of the world. We must make our children top priority. They are our future. Today, the divorce rate is so high. Morality has been degraded to the lowest level ever. We can not have a society of caring and loving children if we are going to turn away from God, who is the giver of life. God is in control of our lives, whether we want to accept that or not. True, we have a free will and can make choices, but without God, we are empty shells just going through life on a constant collision course. We depend solely on ourselves, instead of depending solely on God. Then when we make a bad choice, we wonder why God allowed this to happen to us instead of taking responsibility for our own actions. God gave us children to love and nurture for His Glory, not for the glory of the world.

Many of you may ask what this has to do with the topic. We

must stop allowing ourselves to look for the easy way out. Marriage and children are sacred gifts from God. Today, it is easy and acceptable to walk out on a spouse or family if things go wrong. It takes faith and courage to keep this marriage and family together. There are exceptions to the rule such as; sexual and physical abuse, or alcohol and drug abuse. God did not give us the gift of life to destroy it and make it painful. He gave us life to be lived to the fullest by allowing God to be the Captain guiding our ship. He is the one to depend on in good times and bad.

Being a stepmother has not been a totally joyous experience. Problems arise that are out of a stepparent's control. Sometimes stepparents are not involved in the decision-making process of the children's lives simply because we are the outsiders. Most of the time, all the adults who are involved should put their feelings aside for the best interest of the children. Most of the time, all the adults involved have different God-given talents that can enhance the child's life by making the child feel good about themselves. We are unique in the eyes of God and each of us has so much to offer every child so that they can grow up knowing that they are loved, respected, and positively nurtured to face the tough challenges that this world offers.

They say, "Love conquers all." When was the last time you hugged your child or stepchild? When was the last time you sacrificed your feelings to reach out and to love your child or stepchild unconditionally? When was the last time you and your ex-spouse reassured your children of your love for them? When was the last time all the adults involved sat down a talked calmly about a serious problem that has risen from the behavior of the children? When was the last time all the adults involved honestly made a commitment to one another by doing what is necessary to raise the children in love, peace, respect, and harmony? When was the last time you forgave each other for the suffering that was endured?

I believe the time is now before it is too late. We lost our oldest son to the AIDS virus. There were so many things we could have said, but we did not. Do not let the sun go down without reaching out to your husband, wife, or children and tell them how much you love them and how happy and proud they make you feel. Love can conquer all if only we can put our pride, arrogance and self-centeredness aside. God continues to love us and forgive us no matter how much we hurt Him. Why are we any different?

Now that the stepchildren are older and have become somewhat independent, I sit and look back at how they have matured. I also look at the hurt and misery they are experiencing in their adult lives. I ask myself, "How could I have prevented their pain?" Most divorces cause so much inner confusion to children that will continue to effect them in their adult lives. I know. I am one of those children.

6

MOVING TO LOUISIANA

On July 1, 1986, Jim received a promotion and so we moved to Louisiana. The company flew us to Louisiana to see if we really wanted to accept the promotion. I fought the promotion because the thought of leaving Mom, Sharon, Jim's mother and father, and our Marriage Encounter group was devastating to me. Even though I hated to leave Florida, I put my feelings aside for Jim, who was so excited.

We stayed at the Sheraton Hotel on Canal Street in New Orleans. I remember my first thought was how dirty the city was compared to Florida. I decided to leave the journey in God's hands and keep silent. We stayed for one week and walked through the French Quarter, we ate like pigs, we were driven around by a Realtor to look at apartments, and we rented a car.

I told the Realtor I did not want to live in New Orleans, I wanted to live in the suburbs. The Realtor took us to Metairie, where we found a beautiful two bedroom loft. The apartment was very nice and so was the landlord. We took care of the business at hand, we drove around a while to get acquainted with the area, and went to lunch back at the hotel. Jim was so excited about the entire move. My heart was still in Florida with our family and friends, and our home I really loved. I kept telling myself that God has a reason for this move and I kept trying to put the entire situation in His hands.

When we returned to Florida, Jim accepted the transfer and it was time to sell our home. We made an appointment with a Realtor, who decided that an open house was a good way to begin. During the open house, Jim and I went to the movies. I asked God if it were His Will for us to leave Florida, then let the house sell while we were at the movies. During the movie, at 2:00 P.M., I heard a loud voice in my heart say, "Your house has just been sold." Thinking I was hearing things, I decided to share with Jim what the voice said. He was flabbergasted. After the movie ended, Jim and I raced home to see if what I heard was truth. When we walked into the house, Jim asked the Realtor if she sold the house at 2:00 P.M. She stood their with her month opened, not knowing what to say. When she got her bearings, she told us that one couple came to the open house and they purchased the house on the spot. We shared with her what had happened at the movie and she was shocked. I thought to myself, "God does want us to go. He has plans."

While closing on the house the company sent a moving van to pack us and move us. Meanwhile, our family and friends were happy for us, but yet sad because we were leaving. Jim's children were living up north and could not understand why we would want to leave Florida. Our mothers did not handle the move at all. When we went to say good-bye to his parents and Mom and Sharon, it was devastating. As we were driving away from Mom, she grabbed the window and would not let go. She was hysterical and could not handle the fact we were moving. I told Sharon to take Mom in the house so we could leave. I could feel her heart breaking.

The drive to Louisiana was a quiet one. I could not stop crying. My heart was broken for Mom. We drove straight through and stayed in a hotel when we arrived because we had to wait for the moving van to bring our things.

Finally, we moved into the apartment and settled down to begin our new life. I began sending out resumes for a job, only to hear how poorly the economy was in Louisiana. For every one job, one hundred applicants applied. I was depressed. During the first year of living in Louisiana, I flew back to see Mom and Sharon six times. I hated Louisiana. It reminded me of southern New Jersey.

Since Jim and I were not getting along because I was so miserable, I decided to move back to Florida. Hurt and feeling dejected, Jim agreed it would be best for us to separate. We went to Mass at St Louis King of France in Metairie, which was suppose to be our last Mass together. The Church had confessions before each Mass began. I was so confused, I did not know what to do. I did not want to leave Jim because I loved him so very much, but I knew we could not go on the way we were. All of a sudden a force picked me up onto my feet as if someone was holding my hand and walking me into the confessional. I said, "Ok God, I know it is you and if you have something to say to me then speak through your priest."

Well, God definitely had something to say because the priest let me know under no such terms was it God's Will for me to leave my husband and Louisiana. I accepted it and went back and told Jim what had happened. Confusion set in, and poor Jim did not know if he was coming or going.

I finally got a job with a refrigerator company doing book-keeping work. The job lasted one year because of cut backs. While in Florida on Christmas Eve, the telephone rang with news that Jim's oldest son died from the AIDS virus. Even though we knew he was dying, we still held on to hope and faith that he would be healed. We thanked God that he made peace with Jim before he died. He was a young man who was so kind and compassionate. He loved everyone and everyone loved him. We were all devastated by his death and we prayed that it be God's Will.

I remember a year before his death he and his sister came to visit us in Louisiana. He had lesions all over his body from the AIDS virus. It was summertime and the humidity and heat was horrible. When the children got off the airplane, Jim and I did not recognize his son. He had pancake make-up on his face to cover the lesions and he wore gloves and a long sleeve shirt and long pants to cover his entire body so he would not upset the passengers on the airplane.

When we arrived at the apartment, he put on some comfort-able clothes. Jim and I were devastated at what we saw. He must have weighed 100 pounds. We tried to show both children a good time in New Orleans, but at bedtime, Jim and I would cry in the privacy of our bedroom. The last time we saw Jim's son was when he was built like a football player.

Now he was gone. What a painful way to die. How he loved life, family, and friends. He has been missed, thought of with lov-ing memories, and constantly pray for him. We miss him so very much. There will never be another one like him. Such a loss. Such a tragedy.

Prior to being let go from my job, the issue of abortion came on the television. My boss could see how it upset me. She asked me if I had ever had an abortion. Of course, I replied, "Yes." She told me about how I would make a good volunteer counselor at the

ACCESS Crisis Pregnancy Centers under the auspices of Associated Catholic Charities and the Archdiocese of New Orleans, LA.

I called the telephone number my boss gave me and they wanted to train me as soon as possible. Out of work, with no prospects, I went through the Access training program. It is amazing how God works. The salary I was receiving at the job I lost, my husband was promoted to Supervisor and given an increase in pay that matched the money we lost from my job. We were amazed. Jim told me to volunteer until a prospect for a job came through.

For the first time in my life I loved doing what I was doing. I knew it was the Will of God for this to unfold. One night I had a dream that I was walking in a big open field with Mom. We were talking and laughing. A Heavenly Angel appeared, which I knew was my Guardian Angel, Michael. Michael told me he had to take me somewhere. Mom started crying and begged Michael not to take me from her. Michael told Mom we would be right back. I took Michael's hand and we began to rise toward the clouds. Mom was getting smaller and smaller. She kept crying hysterically and screaming for me to come back.

Michael took me into a room that looked like a movie theater and told me to watch the screen. He then disappeared. On the screen my entire life passed before my eyes, but the main focus was on the abortion experiences. When it was finished, I began to cry. I heard a loud voice say, "If you could change your life would you?" My answer was immediate, "Yes Lord." Michael appeared again and told me he was taking me back to the field. "You must abandon yourself from your mother so you can do the Will of God," the voice said.

The trips to Florida went from six times a year to once a year with Jim. I began going to daily Mass at St. Louis King of France in Metairie, which was down the street from our apartment. On Mondays before Mass, five ladies would get together and clean up the Church by putting the prayer books in each pew rack and collecting the bulletins that were laying all over the place. I felt led to help them.

One Monday I was told by a voice, which I believe was God, to come to 6:30 A.M. Mass and clean the Church before the 8:30

A.M. Mass. So I did. One morning as I was straightening up the Church, I heard a loud voice say, "I am going to gift you with seeing My Mother." I must say I was frightened at first and thought I was losing my mind. Then a peace came over me.

Journalizing all my religious experiences, I wrote this one in the journal when I returned home and then forgot about it. That night I had a dream. I dreamt I was in this big opened field and many people stood around me. To the left of me a woman shouted, "Look at the sun!" So I looked up at the sun which was spinning and changing colors. A Eucharistic Host appeared in the center of the sun and then I saw Our Blessed Mother coming down from the sun that turned into the Host. She was the most beautiful woman I had ever seen. Her garments flowed with the beautiful gentle breeze. I knelt down immediately and began to cry. I told her I loved her and thanked her for this grace and special gift. When I awoke the next morning, I wrote the dream in my journal. That day Father Francis Butler called me to tell me there was a pilgrimage going to Starret, Alabama, where the visionary from Medjugorje, Maria, was recuperating from surgery. Maria gave one of her kidneys to her brother who was very ill. Father Butler told me that Maria walked over to a huge oak tree in the center of a large plowed corn field to receive her apparitions of Our Blessed Mother. Everyone kept telling me that Starret looked like a mini Medjugorje. Father Butler invited me to go and I accepted, even though I did not know anyone. I received a second call from Father telling me that Maria had returned to Medjugorje. I was disappointed. Father said, "Are you going for Maria or Our Blessed Lady?" Father knew how to pierce your heart with truth.

We checked into our rooms and then went to the field to have Mass and have a candlelight procession. Right after Mass, a lady to my left said, "Look at the sun!" I looked up and saw the spinning of the sun. The sun was changing colors. A Eucharistic Host replaced the sun and a beautiful Lady came down from the center of the Host with her garments flowing in a gentle breeze. I fell to my knees and began to cry. I thanked Our Lady for the gift and remembered the dream that took place exactly one month prior to this trip. The dream was exactly how I experienced the gift from

God on the field in Starret. All I could do was Praise God for this beautiful gift. The next morning we returned to the field for Mass. Before Mass began, we walked to the top of the hill to a house that had a gift shop in it and a darkened room with a life size Crucified Jesus. We were not allowed to take pictures. The only light came from the votive candles lit in front of the cross. I knelt down before Jesus in horror. It was the first time I saw a replica of what Jesus looked like on the cross. The hole in His side was not a little slit, it was a hole gouged out the size of a fist. All I could do was cry. I began to sense a form of His suffering, which prevented me from breathing properly. I stared at His wounds as the tears ran down my face. All I could tell Jesus was how sorry I was for what I had done to Him. I thanked Him for dying for me, but I could never repay Him for what He did for me. I just kept telling Him I loved Him.

We left Starret on Sunday after Mass. I could not get Jesus suffering on the cross out of my mind. I knew God had a purpose for this, there was no doubt in my mind. When I returned home, I shared everything with my husband and my friend, Kathy. They told me they were both going on the next trip.

I went back to my daily routine at St. Louis King of France. A couple months had passed. Again, while I was straightening up the Church I heard a loud voice say, "I am going to bless you with seeing My Mother again." That night I dreamt that I was in the field at Starret, Alabama. A woman on my right side shouted out during Mass, "Look there is Mary!" We all looked up on a hill and there she was in all her glory. I ran down the small hill away from everyone. She appeared to me all in white and gold as Our Lady of Fatima. I began to cry. I saw Our Lady lift her right arm with her rosary in her hand sparkling from the sun. I raised my right hand to reach out to her. The next thing I knew Our Lady was standing in front of me in all of her splendor. She told me she wanted to take me somewhere. I asked where and she took a hold of my hand. We went to a place where hundreds of people knew me. I asked her who they were and she told me that they were all of the Holy Souls from Purgatory that I have prayed for. I was shocked. Our Lady impressed on me the importance of praying for the Holy Souls in

Purgatory. This made me happy.

As I stood in heaven a child came running towards me. I knew her. She was beautiful. It was Cecilia, my unborn daughter that I aborted. We held onto one another so tightly. The love radiated between us. I turned to the Blessed Mother and asked if I could stay in heaven because I did not want to go back to the world. Her exact words were, "You have much work to do for My Son. You must go back." My begging for Our Lady to change her mind did not move her. I said good-bye to Cecilia and told her I loved her. Our Lady and I returned to the field. Then she disappeared.

When I awoke by a jolt, I saw in all radiance Gabriel, my unborn son who I aborted, hovering above me. He smiled at me and disappeared. I fell back to sleep very peacefully. I dreamt that Michael, my Guardian Angel, took me to a room in heaven. I sat down and he brought to me Cecelia and Gabriel and placed them in my arms. Michael said to me, "You have not mourned for your loss." He was so right. I have mourned with women and men over their children, but never my own. My children and I cried together, played together, and just loved one another. Once I was at peace, Michael returned to bring me back to the bedroom. I picked up my journal and began to write my experiences down. Of course, I would never forget these dreams. God truly blessed me.

A month to the date of the dreams, Father Butler called and invited me to go to Starret again. This time Jim and Kathy were going too. When we arrived at the field, we began with Mass. After Communion, a woman standing to my right shouted, "Look, there is Mary!" Everyone looked up and there she was. Father Doyle, another priest on the trip, yelled at us and told us to concentrate on the Mass. He said, "If it is Our Blessed Mother up on the hill, she will be there when Mass is completed." He was right. There she was in all her splendor. I ran down to the bottom of the hill. She appeared to me as Our Lady of Fatima. She raised her arm and I saw her rosary sparkling in the sun. I went to raise mine and all of a sudden I heard this loud man's voice say, "Mary is not there. You all are seeing things." I got up and began to walk away. I then heard a beautiful woman's voice say, "Where are you going? Please do not leave me." I turned around and did not see anything and walked away.

I was reminded of the dream I had a month earlier which I documented in my journal. Perhaps Our Blessed Mother was suppose to appear to me as she did in my dream. I will not know until I see her in heaven. I look at both experiences as beautiful gifts from God and I praise Him for them. After these experiences my life was changed forever.

I believe the closer we journey to God, we experience more and more conversion experiences. Each trial or each joy is a conversion experience on the journey to our salvation and our road home to God. We are tested on our journey to see who we will follow, God's Will or the world (Satan).

I have fallen flat on my face so many times I cannot count. Sometimes I think my head is flat instead of round from all the bricks I have been hit with. But from it all the sweet gentle voice keeps saying, "Get up. Shake off the dust and follow me." And each time I do.

7

SURRENDERING TO GOD'S HOLY WILL

One day while I was volunteering for the Access Crisis Pregnancy Center, a young woman walked into the clinic for a free pregnancy test. She was abortion minded. The counselor I was training with showed her a video on an abortion. I was horrified because it was the first time the horror of abortion was placed before my eyes. It took everything I had to keep it together. When the video was over, I began to share with the young woman my experience.

The counselor I was training with looked at me in total shock. The young woman said she could not do this to her baby and left knowing that the truth of abortion was given to her so she could make a choice she could live with.

It was then that I heard a calling to surrender everything in my heart to God. That He wanted to use me as a small vessel of truth and light. "Who else can speak to these women who have experienced the holocaust of abortion and express in truth the tremendous suffering that is endured by a decision that is mainly made in ignorance, fear, or selfishness but you?" God said.

I volunteered for one year. Many babies were being saved from the abortion mill and the babies' mothers, fathers and family members were spared the suffering. In all the years of working with ACCESS, I would never force a woman to believe the way I did. I only shared my story and gave them the true facts so that they could make an informed decision. I always told the women to take three days, to read the materials they were given and to speak to family members and/or friends so they would know before they entered an abortion clinic what was going to take place. They also would know that the baby they were carrying was not a blob of tissue, piece of nothing, or blood clots. The truth was the women were carrying little human beings—babies.

For the first time I found my life had meaning, especially when the women would bring their babies to my office for me to see how beautiful they were. A year later, God started to lead me to begin a "healing ministry" for those women who chose to have an abortion. A refuge of healing so they could be brought back into the loving arms of Jesus. I began investigating the possibilities.

I presented a proposal to the Program Director of ACCESS because I really was not sure of the logistics of the whole program. The proposal was accepted and it would be called the ACCESS Post-Abortion Support Group, which was a seven-week healing program, meeting once a week. Since I had no prior training, the Program Director of ACCESS told me that it was the policy of Associated Catholic Charities for me to be observed by one of their Social Workers for the entire seven weeks. I agreed and began running ads through the Catholic Church Bulletins.

Four women came forward. We used the bible study called "Women in Ramah," which was Nondenominational. We broke the workbook down into seven sections. I could feel the presence of the Holy Spirit with us. It was a miraculous event because I witnessed these women being transformed by God. What a blessing! Even the Social Worker was overwhelmed.

When we completed the seven weeks, the Social Worker informed the agency that I could handle the counseling on my own. She gave me an excellent recommendation, and told me personally that for the first time she realized that since she never experienced an abortion, she could not get beyond a certain level as I could because I experienced an abortion. She also shared the lack of compassion that she noticed in the community for women who experienced an abortion.

Word started getting out in the community. I wrote to priests and nondenominational clergy informing them of this service and I asked them if they would like to be a part of this program. God blessed us with thirty-five priests and five nondenominational clergy.

The Program Director felt it was time to share my experiences at one of the monthly ACCESS volunteer meetings. I was petrified because I flunked Spanish in high school because I would not get up in front of the class, now I am asked to speak. I must have written and rewritten my talk fifteen times. The first four women who completed the program, and the Social Worker who observed me, were present for moral support and to answer any questions. I was scared to death. The podium which I stood behind was rocking and rolling because of my nervousness. After I finished my talk, everyone was crying, clapping, and giving me a standing ovation at the same time. Well, needless to say, I lost it. I asked if they all saw the podium rocking and rolling and could tell I was nervous. They all replied, "No."

It was then that God spoke to my heart and said, "Get used to it. You will be doing a lot of speaking." Of course God is always right. Word got out about my talk and I began speaking publicly in schools, organizations, on the radio and on television. Each time I would be asked to speak, I would solely depend on the Holy Spirit to speak through me. I knew I was a nothing, a simple vessel that God wanted to use for His Greater Glory. It was then I surrendered totally to God and gave Him my life. It is funny in a way, here is a woman who was extremely shy, unable to communicate properly with people, and only had a high school diploma, but she knew to the depths of her soul that only God could bring this all to light.

Public speaking was not easy. Individuals would spit at me, throw things at me, scream at me, call me a murderer, and yet, in all this madness, there I stood totally dependent on God and His Holy Spirit for the wisdom and courage to endure it all. God is so amazing.

Surrendering to God means giving Him all of you so He can use you as a small vessel of truth and light for His Greater Glory. I was a controlling person and did not trust anyone. But God showed me He was not just anyone, He was Love, a love that no human being could ever come close to. He swooped me up in His loving arms and held me close to His bosom and heart of pure, unconditional love and I melted right in His arms.

I always saw God as this elderly man who would punish me if I was bad or He would send bolts of lightning if I did not do what He said or He was just an angry elderly man. Now I know that God is pure, simple, unconditional love. I thank God for allowing me to see Him in His truth and light. I could never purposely try to hurt Him now, even though I am a sinner, not perfect like Jesus, just a sinner who wants to bring joy to God's heart. A sinner that falls on her face because of sin, which does hurt God immensely, but He never stops loving me.

I believe in the Sacrament of Reconciliation or Confession. I remember as a child Mom would take Patricia, Sharon, and I to confession once a month. Confession purifies the soul so you and God can remain united in pure love. A purified soul is as white as fresh snow on a winter's day and smells like a beautiful rose or incense.

I remember my first confession after turning back to God. He blessed me with a very compassionate priest. Before entering the confessional box I said to God, "If this priest represents you, then let Him tell me something that only you know, then I will believe." It is sad how we have to try to test God and be like St. Thomas who doubted Jesus in everything. I just needed a loving affirmation that God was listening. When I finished reciting all my many sins, the priest began telling me thing that only God could have known. I was shocked, amazed, and flabbergasted all in one.

When reciting my penance I told God I would never question His Presence in the confessional again. I believe that the priest is the vessel of God's forgiveness, mercy, and healing. God definitely speaks through the priest and is present during every confession.

I was often told by many holy people that Pope John Paul II goes to confession everyday. This really blew my mind, but in His position, being Peter, the Shepherd of the Roman Catholic Church, he must have a pure heart and soul in constant unity with God. I often wondered what you could confess each day, until my Spiritual Director told me I had to go to confession every week. It was then I truly understood how sinful and dirty my soul was. I always feel free after leaving the confessional. I know that the Holy Spirit, who dwells inside of me, is clean not dirty from sin. It does not matter if the sin is either mortal or venial. Sin is sin. It is not to be sugar-coated. It is to be confessed with a heart that is genuinely sorry for the sins and a heart that will try not to repeat the sins again.

When I counsel someone who has had an abortion experience, whether it be a woman or man, the thing I hear over and over is the tremendous fear of God's punishment and being excommunicated from the Church. Once the individual confesses the sin of abortion, that person is absolved at the moment the priest says, "I absolve you from all your sins, in the name of the Father and of the Son, and of the Holy Spirit." The bottom line of why an individual can not accept God's forgiveness is because they can not forgive themselves for what they have done.

It is like an open sore that festers and festers until medicine is put on it so the sore can heal. This concept is the same when it comes to abortion. Until someone is ready to seek counseling to be healed, the sore with continue to fester. When you can not forgive yourself, you can not accept God's forgiveness. It usually takes an average of ten years before an individual will seek any form of counseling and God's help. Sometimes, a professional therapist will tell an individual, "The experience is over, get over it, go on with your life because there is nothing you can do about the experience or change it." These professionals do not have the vaguest idea of what an abortion does to a woman or anyone involved in the experience.

That is why I am a firm believer in self help programs like Alcoholics Anonymous. The program is centered in God and it is structured where alcoholics help alcoholics.

Abortion is controversial and many disagree with me which is fine. But I am asked by everyone who calls for help if I experienced an abortion. When I tell them yes, there is a peace that comes over them that they will not be judged or condemned. They will be embraced, loved, and understood in a very compassionate way. If there is a case that goes beyond the abortion issue such as molestation, incest or rape, physical or mental abuse, or other relational problems other then abortion, I immediately make referrals to a professional or a priest.

I can only speak for myself when I say, when I am confronted with trials or dark times of the world which I find difficult to handle on my own and prayer is not bringing me solace, I find solace in speaking with a priest. It is in the compassion of the priest that I can see Jesus Christ who speaks through the priest to answer all my questions.

The saddest thing that hurts my heart the most is how priests are condemned and the Roman Catholic Church is persecuted by the media. Sometimes I feel that the media does the dirty work for the evil one, and how much joy it must bring him. They only speak the truth when it suits them best or it is the popular thing to say. On abortion, the media deceives people whenever they get their chance. The average pro-life person is prayerful and stands for the right to life from the moment of conception to natural death. And yes, there are a few individuals who go beyond what being pro-life means. Killing an abortionist is not of God, that is taking one life for another. We, as pro-life people, can not play God. We are on this earth to serve God, not by murdering His children. So you have two choices, either stand with God in truth and light or stand with the Evil One or the world in deceptions and lies. I prefer to stand in truth and light with God. I was once on the other side and look what happened to me. A life filled with anger, hatred, confusion, deception and rhetoric. Whoever thought of the campaign of calling people pro-choice, must have thought she or he was a genius. I believe that we are all pro-choice. There are those of us who choose life (pro-life), and the rest who choose death (pro-death).

My husband has drilled in my head, only good comes from God. Jim did not know how profound he was. Abortion is not from God, nor does He make exceptions to the law. God's law is that every life is a gift from Him—from conception to natural death. Another law is—we are to be chaste whether God sends us a spouse to love and procreate or have children or if God call us to be single. He does not make exceptions for those who want to live whatever lifestyle they wish to live. We are to be chaste as single people, as well as married people. We should be honored to please God and be chaste in union with Him. Surrendering your entire life to God by taking the vow of chastity, single or married, would be the greatest gift you can give to God.

After one year, the ACCESS Post-Abortion Support Group left Associated Catholic Charities and became a part of the Louisiana Pro-life Council. We then named the program S.A.V.E. (Suffering Abortion Victims Embraced) and established the seven-week healing program on February 13, 1989. One year later, Archbishop

Schulte requested that we return to Associated Catholic Charities, where we remained until our departure on December 31, 1995.

Since our establishment, we have helped 475 women, 10 men, 10 grandparents to the unborn, 3 family members, and 2 friends find peace, forgiveness, healing, and a closer walk with Christ, we helped 2,000 women in crisis pregnancies, helped to save 1,800 babies from being aborted, and spoke publicly to over 2 million people on Post-Abortion Syndrome.

On September 27, 1995, S.A.V.E. was incorporated in the state of Louisiana and remains that way to this day.

8

JOSEPHINA MARIA—VISIONARY FROM AUSTRALIA

Josephina-Maria is a visionary from Australia. She has been approved by her Bishop, and travels throughout the world speaking about the two hearts—the Sacred Heart of Jesus and the Immaculate Heart of Mary. She has apparitions of both Jesus and Mary and has started a convent in Australia, plus she has also started a third order lay ministry of the two hearts.

On October 25, 1995, Josephina-Maria came to St. Margaret Mary Catholic Church in Slidell, Louisiana, which was our parish at the time. I kept sensing all through the day the importance of Jim and I staying after Mass to hear her talk. While in the bathroom, procrastinating if I really wanted to attend, I heard a very loud voice say, "It is My Holy Will that you attend this important event. For I, the Father Almighty has a calling for you if you choose to say yes."

Upon hearing this voice, I began to discern if it was really the voice of God, so I asked for an affirmation. I call affirmations apples or oranges, which is a slang term I use to get my questions answered by heaven. An apple or orange can be a certain color of rose, a butterfly, a bird, a color of clothing on someone who may walk through the door when you are in the Eucharistic Adoration Chapel and etc. An affirmation is something you do internally and silently in the depths of your heart to ask the voice you hear if it is really coming from heaven and to give you a sign. This discernment is done silently, so that the Evil One can not hear what is being said in the depths of our hearts. Speaking the affirmation aloud, the Evil One can trick us into believing that the voice was from heaven, when it really came from hell. I really have asked for apples and oranges by the way. Surprisingly, I received them. You can even ask for more than one. Most people pray the St. Therese of Lisieux five day novena. By the fifth day, St. Therese will send you a rose, only if God approves your request. If it is no, you will not receive a rose.

Well needless to say I received my affirmation. Being as hard headed as I can be, I asked for another one and received that too. So off Jim and I went to hear the visionary. Mass came first before the talk and it was so powerful that we could feel the Holy Spirit so strongly. After Mass, Josephina-Maria began to speak. Her talk was so intense that I focused in on every word she was saying, especially the messages from Jesus and Mary. Basically, she shared with us the same things as other visionaries around the world. Prayer, penance, fasting, daily Mass, and monthly Reconciliation (confession).

In her talk she began to speak about the "victim soul." There was a surge or force that pierced my heart and I began to cry uncontrollably. I then heard this loud voice again. He said, "I have chosen you to be my 'victim soul' for the end of abortion, especially for the mothers, fathers, and others who have suffered tremendously from the experience and the conversion of the abortionists who treat my children with the coldest of hearts just to make money. This is dehumanizing to Me. For all life is a gift from Me."

In my heart I knew this was my purpose for being at the Mass and talk, and I knew I was hearing the voice of God. As I listened more intently to Josephina-Maria, she explained what a "victim soul" was. A "victim soul" is an individual who, chosen by God and approved by a Spiritual Director, is asked to take on the sufferings of others and be willing to physically die for the salvation of that individual(s) soul or salvation. God is the one who chooses who the "victim soul" will suffer and die for. This suffering vocation is done with great humility, silence, and always for the greater glory of God.

I heard the voice say, "Will you do this for Me and My Greater Glory?" I contemplated what the voice was asking me. Fear wreaked through my body. Then a rush of fire from the Holy Spirit entered. I said, "Yes," but I did not surrender my heart. At the end of Josephina-Maria's talk, Father Joseph Benson and Josephina-Maria had relics of the True Cross, which is a piece of the cross that Jesus Christ was crucified on. We all formed a line to kiss the relic, which was encased in a crucifix. After kissing the cross, Father Benson and Josephina-Maria prayed over each of us with the "True Cross." I fell slain in the Spirit, which means an individual is overwhelmed by the power of the Holy Spirit and falls to the floor peacefully resting in the Holy Spirit. It is a time the Holy Spirit speaks to you or you speak to Him. Other heavenly beings may even speak to you.

While lying peacefully with the Holy Spirit, He appeared to me and said, "Do not be afraid. For all of heaven is with you. You will suffer emotionally, physically, and spiritually, but you will never be alone." All of a sudden I felt this enormous peace enter me and I said, "YES" to God in total surrender, love, peace, and a pure heart.

I had been controlling my life for a long time. It was time for me to surrender and do the Will of God, then I would be opened to allow God to use me as a vessel in any way He chose.

After a couple of days of letting this experience sink into my mind and heart, and honestly and humbly accepting the Will of God and His call, I met with Father Benson to share with him what had happened. He was elated as he discerned what I was sharing. He then told me that he believed I was chosen by God for this suffering vocation because it tied into the healing ministry I was doing for God already. Father Benson did not want me to obsess over the vocation, nor let pride or arrogance set into my heart and mind. "Stay focused," Father Benson said. He emphatically told me to just surrender all of me to God and allow God to tell me what His Will was and how and when I will suffer. Father Benson continued to tell me to try to be as silent as possible, until God gives me the word to share the experience with others. I walked away from our meeting refreshed and filled with joy.

Being in a healing ministry for those who experienced abortion, I could more intently feel the sufferings of those I had been directing in the S.A.V.E. (Suffering Abortion Victims Embraced) ministry or program for the past six years (at the time of this experience).

When it comes to abortion and the killing of a child, psychologically one can deny or justify their actions, but spiritually, I believe, one has a breakdown in faith, hope, and trust in God. I believe, when the body is psychologically and spiritually impaired, anything destructive can happen, especially when you are accepting everything the world is telling you. It is a constant battle between good, which is God, and evil, which is Satan and the world.

I have heard people say that choosing abortion is an easy choice. I say to those individuals, you have not walked the walk or talked the talk. Everything inside a woman tells her abortion is wrong. The woman is fearful, weak, and is seeking help from someone, anyone. Does she go to the correct places to find the truth? Not always. Most women just go to abortion clinics and accept what they are told. It is afterwards that their actions and decisions hit them smack in the face and then it is too late. The abortion experience is so traumatic that a woman will never forget the experience for the rest of her life. This traumatic experience can effect men, grandparents to the unborn, family members, and friends also.

When I counsel individuals affected by abortion, God blesses me with seeing the individuals heart through the power of His Holy Spirit. I thought my abortion experience was devastating. It does not ever compare to the many other individuals I have counseled with. We do have one common goal, we desire strongly in being united with God by allowing His unconditional love, His mercy, and His forgiveness to penetrate our hearts, our minds, and our souls. Then we can be totally healed and made whole again.

When we stand in truth and light of God, we have a different perspective on life and the gift of life. I believe the majority of women who are pro-abortion or pro-death are fighting for the right to choose by allowing the suffering of abortion to continue. Most of these women have experienced an abortion and are trying to justify their actions.

If only we would turn to God for all of our needs, good and bad, trials and joys, and trust in Him explicitly by doing His Will, then the suffering that we have brought on ourselves will not occur because He loves each of us so much that He will not leave us where we are, wallowing in self-destructive behavior.

Jesus suffered excruciating pain and died on the cross all for the love of God the Father and us. He did this for us so that we would be saved. We can repay Jesus by loving Him and trying to live a sinless life by valuing life from the moment of conception to natural death. We can repay Jesus by getting involved and taking a stand for life. The best spokesperson for pro-life are those who have had an abortion experience. We can repay Jesus by praying constantly for the world and the end of abortion. And we can repay Jesus by lifting every suffering, trial, and joy up for the greater glory of God without complaint. We can not get to heaven unless we suffer here on earth. There is no other way. If Jesus got there that way, why should we be any different?

In His Truth and In His Light

9

ST. IGNATIUS SPIRITUAL EXERCISES

I attended the Spiritual Exercises of St. Ignatius of Loyola at St. Margaret Mary Catholic Church in Slidell, Louisiana. Msgr. Richard Carroll, the Pastor of the Church, had a vision of offering classes on different topics related to educating the participants on the teachings of the Roman Catholic Church. Monsignor Carroll's vision went beyond just education, the participants were to use the knowledge they received to evangelize our brothers and sisters who had fallen away from the Roman Catholic Church. The classes consisted of spiritual growth exercises, Church doctrine, Bible studies, and etc.

Monsignor Carroll also had a religious experience of hearing the Blessed Virgin Mary speak to him, as if to a child, inviting him to prepare St. Margaret Mary to become God's Remnant Church. Monsignor Carroll wrote a book called, "The Remnant Church." The Remnant was a catalyst for preparing for the "Triumph of the Immaculate Heart of Mary," which we are presently living. We will discuss this in a later chapter.

The St. Ignatius Exercises take you to a plateau of your life and total union with God. The exercises have you read a scripture reading and contemplate on it by visualizing yourself in the reading. For example the Birth of Jesus. You can visualize yourself as one of the shepherds that the angel appeared to or standing in the background of the stable watching Jesus being born. It is through your imagination that God speaks to you. After the image is over, you write your experience in your journal.

The book we used for the class was, "A-Do-It-At-Home-Retreat—The Spiritual Exercises of St. Ignatius of Loyola," by Andre Ravier, S.J. A few of the exercise topics consisted of desolation and consolation of the soul, how does God really see us or how do we see ourselves, death, and etc. The topic that affected me the most was the topic on death. The chapter on death had three desires that you could request. I requested to be taken to heaven, to purgatory, and to hell. I asked Jesus to hold one hand and my Guardian Angel, Michael, to hold the other hand. I could feel their presences with me and them holding my hands. We began to descend into total darkness. I remember my eyes were open and it appeared to me like we were on an elevator and I could see the entrances to each floor as you do on a real elevator. When we stopped, we were in the pit of hell surrounded by fire. I became sick to my stomach from the horrible smell of urine and sulfur. The smell was definitely nothing I ever smelled before. I saw these grotesque black translucent demons finding pleasure tormenting souls. The souls were screaming all kinds of obscenities at Jesus. I asked if I could comfort them. As I went to step forward a very strong force held me back. Jesus said, "You were brought here to witness. Now where do you want to go?" I answered, "Purgatory."

I could literally feel myself rising with both Jesus and Michael still holding my hands. When we arrived in purgatory, the Blessed Mother was giving water to the Holy Souls there. I turned and asked Jesus if I could help His mother and He approved. As I gave them water, I would pray with them and talk to them. They asked me to continue to be faithful in my constant prayer for them because it was so important to them. Our prayers release them into heaven, which they desire so much. I remember purgatory being hot with the fire of the desire for heaven. It was a place of purification or atonement of sin. We must be totally purified before we can enter the Kingdom of God. As I saw different levels of hell, I also saw different levels of purgatory.

Jesus then asked me what my third and last desire was. I told Him I wanted to go to heaven where the aborted babies were. When we arrived, at what seemed like a cathedral, I was horrified at the millions of children that were there. When you hear the number 35 million abortions since Roe vs. Wade, it is hard for us to comprehend until we see them for ourselves. I felt so overwhelmed that I began to cry uncontrollably. Jesus told me to come and sit down with Him. As we were walking over to a bench, my children, Cecilia, Gabriel, and Sarah were holding onto me. They told me not to cry, but I could not control it. Each child wanted me to hold them. They surrounded me. They were all so beautiful that I could not take my eyes off of their radiance of love. I put my head on Jesus' lap and asked Him what He wanted me to do so that the killing of these innocent children would not continue. Jesus asked, "What would you like to do?" I told Jesus whatever God's Will was. He then asked me, "Would you suffer and physically die for the unborn who are threatened to be aborted, for their mothers and fathers, their grandparents and other family members, and their friends, and for the conversion of the abortionists and staff?" I said, "YES," immediately. I embraced my children and our love for each other was so comforting.

I returned to my room, totally peaceful. I knew the suffering I had already begun to endure would intensify as time went on. I knew in my heart that the suffering was also for my salvation. I continued the S.A.V.E. Healing Ministry, counseling individuals and publicly speaking on Post-Abortion Syndrome by sharing my testimony and the testimonies of others. The ignorance, selfishness, and lack of compassion was at times, more than I could endure. But I pressed on for all those babies I saw and especially for the love of God. I never really knew God before these exercises. The exercises helped me to love God in a deeper way. St. Ignatius took me to the depths of my soul, preparing me for what was ahead of me as I traveled down the path to God's purpose for my life—a small vessel or instrument that God needed to use to hopefully change hearts.

The truth and light of God is a path that is not easy. You will have hills and valleys, twists and turns, and bumps and bruises. But most of all you have persecution and betrayal from people who believe you to be true, but out of jealousy, label you as a fake or a fraud. A very wise person told me, "If you want to be totally humble, you must lose your reputation."

What does this mean? It means your focus must remain on the cross always, and you can not allow what people say to hurt you or to destroy you. Once you accept the hurt, anger, and other negative feelings, you have lost the battle. By nature, most if not all human beings are judgmental, condemning, gossipy, and/or curious. If you keep your eyes on Jesus, all that is going on around you will never effect you because Jesus will not allow others to distract you from what God has called or asked you to do. It is when we take our eyes off of Jesus and the cross, that we fall flat on our face because we open ourselves up to be persecuted, which comes from Satan and the world, not God. ONLY GOOD COMES FROM GOD.

I kept a journal on the many wonderful things that I experienced through the St. Ignatius exercises. I thank and praise God for this beautiful gift He blessed me with. I highly recommend the exercises to everyone. The Bible has become more alive to me now because I can meditate on each scripture reading or story by placing myself in each one. There are many people who have a difficult time visualizing. Just depend on the power of the Holy Spirit. Ask Him to make the Bible come alive by taking you on the journey. The Holy Spirit moves with each person in different ways. Remember, we are all unique and different in God's eyes. Not one of us is the same. If you have the opportunity, please look into attending a St. Ignatius class or purchasing the book and asking your Spiritual Director or a priest to assist you.

The St. Ignatius Exercises enhanced my faith in God. It is a tool that is theologically sound and enriched spiritually. If done properly, your life will never be the same. Your journey with God will only become more humble, peaceful, and enriched by the power of God's unconditional love for you.

Through the power of the Holy Spirit and the help of some knowledgeable and loving priests, we published the S.A.V.E. (Suffering Abortion Victims Embraced) Roman Catholic Healing manuals for Women, Men, Grandparents to the Unborn, Family Members and Friends, since 98% of our clients were Roman Catholic. The results have been astounding.

10

A DEEPER CALL TO SUFFERING

On October 19, 1996, I was leaving New Orleans, Louisiana for Medjugorje, Yugoslavia, which is now called Croatia—Hersekovenia. Medjugorje is the place where Our Blessed Mother began appearing in 1981 to six children. The children are now grown, with five married and one, Vitska, still single. The war surrounds the village, but Medjugorje remains untouched even to the present time.

Monsignor Carroll was suppose to be our Spiritual Director on the trip, but at the last minute he could not go because he broke his toe which became infected. He begged his doctor to let him go, but his doctor still refused because if the infection got worse, he could die. Disappointed, Monsignor Carroll turned to Our Blessed Mother, but received no approval. It was not the Will of God. The group was disappointed, especially me because Monsignor Carroll had become my Spiritual Father. He was the only one out of a few people who loved me and showed me respect no matter what I had done in the past. I looked up to him like a little child.

Five of us from the parish were going on the pilgrimage and we met in the parish parking lot. Monsignor Carroll sent us off our way with his blessing. We were all crying because he was not coming with us. Pat Dougherty and her son were kind enough to drive us to the airport. When we arrived at the airport, Father Greene, our Spiritual Director for the pilgrimage and the others from the group had already arrived. Everyone introduced themselves and an excitement filled the air.

We flew from New Orleans, Louisiana, to Houston, Texas, then onto Chicago, Illinois, via Continental Airlines. We then flew from Chicago to Paris, France via Air France. When we arrived in Paris, we caught a flight that stopped at Zagraf first, then continued to our final airline destination of Split. Even though we were taking the same airplane from Zagraf to Split, we were told that when the airline changes crew members, the passengers must get off the plane and go through customs. When our group completed customs, we boarded a bus to take us back to the plane.

When we arrived in Split, we had a bus and tour guide, Anna, waiting for us for our long drive to Medjugorje. The trip was tiring, but our group was so enjoyable to be with.

When we finally arrived at the home where we were staying, we were all excited and could not sleep. The five pilgrims from St. Margaret Mary, (Jackie, Yvonne, Shirley, Andre, and myself) decided to walk to St. James Church which was five minutes away. My roommate was Shirley, a very loving woman and mother who lost her daughter, Maria, months before the trip to leukemia. My heart went out to her, especially when she cried because she missed Maria so much. Shirley's other children paid for her trip. The strange thing was none of us knew one another, but we acted like we had been friends forever.

On this spiritual journey, Jackie and I became very close, almost more like sisters than friends. We knew Our Blessed Mother had brought us together. We had love and mutual respect for each other which we believed was a gift from Our Lady. We treasure this relationship to this day. Jackie and I were slow walkers and had difficulty keeping up with Father Greene. Every morning Father Greene climbed either Cross Mountain or Apparition Hill before most of us woke up. He was amazing. Jackie, Yvonne, Shirley, and I decided to walk slow so we could enjoy everything. Yvonne took pictures of she and the goats. It was hysterical.

We began our journey up Apparition Hill. This was the place where Our Blessed Mother appeared to the six children until the authorities prevented it. Then the children were moved to a room at St. James Church. Yvonne could not climb the hill, so she stayed at the bottom of the hill and made friends or pen pals as she called them. Yvonne is a people person, a beautiful light of God and a teacher. She attracts people to her and can communicate with everyone she meets. The people loved her.

Medjugorje was beautiful. It was the first time I had ever visited a foreign country. Jackie, Shirley, and I began to climb Apparition hill. As you climb the hill there are bronze etchings of the fifteen decades of the rosary. We climbed and prayed at the same time. As we completed the Joyful Mysteries of the rosary, we arrived at the first level of the hill. We walked over to a large wooden cross on top of a large pile of rocks. I knelt down in front of the cross and prayed. When I completed my prayer, I heard a voice say, "Take a picture now!" I got up, snapped a picture, and went on with my prayer. I found a place on a large rock to sit and continue to pray. The peace that was there was indescribable. The quietness was embraceable and the sound of the wind was such a blessing. As I looked over the countryside I could understand why Our Blessed Mother chose this place, Medjugorje, as her special place to appear. The people were so humble. They have very little and what they do have they share with the millions of pilgrims that come there on a continuous basis. The pilgrims have shown their generosity by bringing money, gifts, and medical supplies.

As I continued to sit on the rock, I heard the sweet voice again say, "Move over to a quieter place. I have a message for you from God." I moved over to another large rock on the hill and heard and received a message which I wrote in my journal dated October 21, 1995. The message in summary was a call to a deeper suffering and being called to be a "victim soul" was spoken again. I thanked and praised the voices, whom I believe was God the Father and Our Blessed Mother. I also received a short message for Jackie, whom the Blessed Mother called Jacqualine. Jacqualine was overwhelmed with the message and told me it was authentic because that is her true name, which I did not know.

On October 22, 1995, the group climbed Cross Mountain. The small rocks became boulders. It was so difficult to climb and yet so peaceful. The bronze etchings going up the mountain were the Stations of the Cross and so we said them as a group. When we arrived on the top of the mountain, the view was magnificent. The cross was huge and the peace pierced my heart and soul. Once again I was asked by the sweet voice to go off to a quiet place alone and receive another message, which I did. It was time to leave the mountain, but I did not want to leave because it seemed like we had just arrived. Our Lady was walking with me and talking to me so clearly. I was so upset to leave so suddenly because I knew I could not climb this mountain again. Walking down the mountain was difficult because of the rough terrain. People were passing me with bare feet and I thought what a blessing and sacrifice for God. Jacqualine and I walked back to the house where we were staying alone. We talked and talked. It was wonderful. She is such a beautiful, humble, and holy woman. She made the pilgrimage the most memorable of my life. The group visited Vicka, whom I always loved so much. She is the visionary that radiates love and the one whose light has shown the most when it came to Our Blessed Mother. When she spoke, you could see Our Blessed Mother in her and you knew Our Blessed Mother was with her. After Vicka spoke to us, she asked us to bow our heads and pray with her. She also requested that we not take pictures. Everytime I lifted my head, Vicka caught me and we smiled at each other. Her holiness overpowered me, but I knew it was the power of the Holy Spirit I was seeing in her eyes and on her face. It was the total surrendered love to God and the Blessed Mother.

After hearing Maria and Father Slosovich speak, we heard Vicka. They both reiterated what Vitska had told us. It was then I realized that I did not come to Medjugorje to hear what the visionaries had to say, I came to be in communion with God through the intercession of the Immaculate Heart of Mary.

I went to Mass everyday at 9:00 A.M. The Church was packed and I had to sit on the floor. After receiving Jesus on October 24, 1995, the sweet voice told me to climb Apparition Hill one more time. This time by myself. The group was going to Dubrovinec, so I told them I would not be going with them. Jacqualine asked me what I was going to do and I told her what the sweet voice said to me. Jacqualine asked if she could join me on the climb up the hill and she would leave me alone. I sensed it was fine with Our Blessed Mother and so off we went. As we began to climb the hill, we decided to slowly say our rosary, stopping at each bronze etching, while sitting down on a rock meditating on each Joyful Mystery. When we got to the fourth mystery, the Presentation of Our Lord, I began to see a form in the etching. It was God the Father with the Holy Spirit hovering over God's head. The sweet voice told me to take a picture, which I did.

When we arrived at the first landing, we separated. Once again

I heard the sweet voices speaking to me as I wrote their words in my journal. The message was affirming the importance of me attending daily Mass and receiving the Holy Eucharist, one hour of Eucharistic Adoration each week, fasting on Fridays, prayer, living simple, being obedient, being humble, going to the Sacrament of Reconciliation more than once a month, and suffering for the Roman Catholic Church and for abortion.

When I completed my message, I received another for Jacqualine. Jacqualine and I went off to a quiet place where we would not disturb the others who were focused on prayer. I shared both messages with Jacqualine. While I was reading them to her, a beautiful butterfly landed on the journal, then it landed on Jacqualine, and then on me. This took place during the entire reading of both messages. When I completed reading the messages, the butterfly disappeared, but not before Jacqualine took a picture of it. We believed it was Our Blessed Mother affirming the messages and telling us that we have surrendered to heaven and we were given a new life in God.

On October 25, 1995, the group visited the cemetery where Masses were being held during the war. Jacqualine and I decided to remain in the cemetery for some time, instead of going with the group. The peace and silence was staggering. As I was praying I was looking up at Cross Mountain in the distance. The Cross suddenly began to spin and then disappeared. Our Blessed Mother appeared to me and began to speak about her love for me and God's love for me. She spoke, I listened. She was so beautiful. I did not want to leave Medjugorje. The picture of God the Father and the Holy Spirit, which was on the etching of the Presentation of the Lord, appeared in the picture, as did the butterfly Jacqualine took, and Our Blessed Mother appeared in the picture I took before the wooden cross with a women lying on the rocks holding onto the cross.

Controversy has errupted over the authenticity of Medjugorje. I know what I experienced was from God and I really do not care what anyone else thinks. Jacqualine was there with me during it all and not once did she disbelieve what was taking place. I Praise God and Our Blessed Mother for these wonderful and special gifts and graces they gave to Jacqualine and I. What we experienced in Medjugorje, was in the truth and light of God.

After the Medjugorje trip, I was blessed with traveling to Guadalupe, Mexico, with my sister, Sharon. We were going for the Feast Day of Our Lady of Guadalupe. During the Feast Day Mass, December 12, 1996, I heard babies crying. It overwhelmed me to hysteria. The trip was a blessing from God and affirmed again the calling from God. The thing that impressed me the most about the Mexican people was their true devotion to Our Lady of Guadalupe. As we were visiting different towns each day, we would see people and families walking miles and miles to make sure they attended one of the many Masses that were taking place around the clock for the Feast Day. Their devotion brought sadness to my heart because of the lack of devotion in the United States. The Mexican people are humble, simple people who love Our Blessed Mother so very much. Unlike most people of the United States who are materialistic. The trip consisted of forty people with Father Joseph Benson as our Spiritual Director. It was a wonderful trip and the pilgrims made this trip memorable also.

On April 12, 1997, I was called to Italy by St. Francis of Assisi and St. Padre Pio. After Mass, as I knelt down at the tomb of St. Francis of Assisi, he reiterated the call of suffering from God. It was on this trip I learned that St. Francis and St. Therese were my Patron Saints.

At the tomb of St. Francis, he told me to go to the gift shop because he had a special gift for me. So, I entered the gift shop, which was not well lit, looked around and exited. As I began to walk away, I heard a loud voice say, "Go back to the gift shop." "Ok," I replied. I entered the gift shop for the second time and was directed to the rosaries hanging on a rack. As I was going through the rosaries, I felt a presence next to me. The rosaries began to move and one was placed in my hand. I thought I was losing my mind. I paid for the rosary, dipped it in the Holy Water fount as I was exiting the Cathedral and handed it to Father Benson to bless. I then returned to my seat. I heard Father Benson say, "What a beautiful rosary!" I thought he was crazy. When he returned the gift from St. Francis back to me, I looked at it very closely and began to cry. The rosary was gold with red beads the color of blood. I cried and cried. The rosary was magnificent and I realized that what Father Benson said was true. The rosary was beautiful.

As we toured Assisi, I learned more about St. Francis's suffering and His unprecedented relationship with God. St. Francis, because of His love, poverty, humility, obedience, charity, chastity, and tremendous suffering, passed through the threshold to God, which I spoke of in the introduction. God the Father appeared to him on his retreat and granted him two desires. It was then Francis received the stigmata or the five wounds of Jesus Christ.

Assisi was magnificently breathtaking. We visited the little Church of St. Francis, San Domiano, where the Crucified Jesus appeared to St. Francis on a cross, and the caves where St. Francis prayed. What an awesome place to pray. We visited other places associated with him too. We also visited The Church of St. Clare, where her body is incorrupt, which means her dead body remained intact. The skin on her face looked a little leathery, but it was amazing to see how beautifully peaceful she was.

We then went to the Monastery of the Benedictines. The monastery was beyond words. I told everyone to leave me alone, I just wanted to be in silence with God. When we entered the monastery the monks were singing their Divine Office. It was like we were in heaven listening to the choir of angels singing and chanting to glorify God. As I walked around the Church, I came upon the Eucharistic Adoration Chapel, knelt down and prayed for a while. What an awesome experience. The grounds were embraceable. I was going to ask the monks if I could stay, but it was time to go.

Our journey continued to San Giovanni. We went to the Rotundo where Padre Pio's tomb is located. We had Mass at the tomb and then we went on a tour through the Rotundo with Father Joseph, a Capuchin Monk who lived there. We learned how Padre Pio suffered from the stigmata, the five wounds of Jesus Christ. He also suffered silently, asking for no consolation. I remember saying to myself that I am such a whimp compared to Padre Pio. As we approached the cell of Padre Pio, which was enclosed in glass, I heard a voice say, "My gift to you is to show my face in this picture when you have the film developed." I snapped the picture and went on with the tour. The peace was tremendous there. The time spent in San Giovanni was so healing and powerful.

While there, the group did the Stations of the Cross, which wrapped around part of the mountain. The etchings were in bronze and were so intense and so humble. As we went from station to station the contemplative suffering of Jesus was heartrending. Then when we saw Jesus hanging on the cross, I wept and contemplated that moment in time, standing at the foot of the cross weeping with His mother, Mary, Mary Magdalen, and John. I never experienced the Stations of the Cross in such a powerful way before. When the pictures were developed, the face of Padre Pio was included in the picture of his room. What a blessing!

We spent a couple of days in San Giovanni before returning to Rome. When we arrived in Rome, we toured the ruins and other places of interest. The group and thousands of others had tickets to the audience with Pope John Paul II, whom I love, pray for, and follow. I truly believe that the Pope was hand picked by Our Blessed Mother. The Pope's devotion to Our Blessed Mother is so loving and deeply moving. As the Pope rode by in his Pope-mobile, I snapped a picture. It was always my dream to be close to the Pope. I always wanted to give him the biggest hug of love. We spent a couple of days in Rome and visited the many Roman Catholic Churches there. The Church that impressed me was St. Mary Major. St. Mary Major had relics in it. Relics are pieces of the human body, manly bones of the Saints encased in glass. In one glass encasing there was a portion of the "True Cross," the finger St. Thomas stuck in Jesus' side to see if it was really Jesus when He appeared to the apostles after the Resurrection, two of the thorns from the Crown of Thorns that Jesus wore, one of the nails that was used to crucify Jesus, and a few other relics. We could feel the True Presence. It was overwhelming. When we walked into the other room and the light went on, there were relics of hundreds of Saints. We were so humbled and honored to be in their presence. How awesome! It was time to leave to return to the United States.

God is so good when He blesses us with gifts and graces. Each pilgrimage was part of my journey of salvation, of love, and of the union with God the Father, Jesus, the Holy Spirit, the Blessed

Mother, the Holy Saints and Holy Angels. The trips will be in my memory and heart forever. The pictures that I was blessed with are kept in a separate folder so they can be looked at and praise God for all His wondrous gifts to me.

In His Truth and In His Light

11

THE SPIRITUAL UNKNOWN—
SPIRITUAL WARFARE

Spiritual Warfare is dealing with the realm of good and evil spirits. All of us have a good side and dark side. That is why we are sinners. As we grow closer to God, our sinfulness becomes more and more appalling to us because sin is appalling to God. ALL SIN. That is why we, as Roman Catholics, go to the Sacrament of Reconciliation (confession), to cleanse our souls, hearts, and minds of the filth that builds up inside of us. We become dirty, instead of remaining pure and this is the time when we are the most vulnerable or open to evil and sin. When we receive absolution from a priest, we are made pure and white as snow until we sin again. I believe, the Sacrament of Reconciliation is one of our greatest sacraments. The greatest of course, is receiving the Body and Blood, Soul and Divinity of Jesus Christ in the Eucharist.

The tempter and temptress of sin is Satan and Jezebel. We are tempted constantly to do bad and be disobedient by rejecting the Will of God. A very wise priest, Father Ken Harney, once told me during Spiritual Direction, "Linda, God gives us two paths to choose, God's Will or the world (Satan). God will show us both paths and what each path has to offer. If we choose God's Will, God will show us the hills and valleys, but at the end is Paradise. If we choose the world, we accept the lust, power, greed, materialism, arrogance, and everything that goes with it. The choice is ours because of the free will God has given us." Since then every decision I have to make, I take directly to God.

Another very wise man who was the instrument in bringing me to God the Father is Bishop Nicholas D'Antonio. We call him Bishop Nick. Bishop Nick said to me, "Linda, every time you have a negative thought, lift it up to God immediately. Then the thought becomes a constant prayer and the evil one has no power over you." Think how many times a day we have negative thoughts. We could be praying constantly to God even in our trials. Believe me, God does turn the negative thought into a positive one.

My first encounter with the dark side was at age three when I was molested and saw horrible scary monsters. But in my adult life the first time I experienced the true power of the realm of spiritual warfare was when Jim and I first moved to Louisiana. Jim had to travel alot with his job and I was home alone. Afraid of the dark as far back as childhood, I would see things and have to sleep with a night-light. I still do to this day.

The night before Jim was coming home from a trip, I sensed something evil standing in the corner of our bedroom. I prayed and prayed, but it would not leave. I ended up on the couch watching television until the sun came up. The night Jim arrived home, we went to sleep and I was awakened by a force that was so strong that it elevated me off the bed. Looking down at Jim and screaming, he remained fast asleep. The thing had me by my thighs and began thrashing me around. I was horrified. When the thing was gone, I woke up Jim to tell him what happened. Jim was skeptical of course, until I showed him my thighs. There were ten small bruises in the shape of finger tips, five on each thigh. I cried and cried because I did not understand what I had done for this to happen.

We called our friend, more like a brother, Father David Rabe, a Theologian at Notre Dame Seminary and the Spiritual Director for S.A.V.E., INC., the post-abortion healing program. He came over immediately to exorcise the apartment in Latin and English, and to bless and to pray over Jim and I. He saw the bruises, which really shook him up. He told me that he believed because of the ministry God had called me to, S.A.V.E., that Satan was furious and wanted to scare me. He also told me I must be doing something right if Satan has become this brutal.

Since that time many encounters with the demonic have taken place. Satan has appeared in all forms. He has tried so hard to virtually scare me to death. Praise God that he has not been successful. I thought I was crazy when it came to all of this spiritual warfare stuff, until I heard about Padre Pio's encounters with Satan. St. Padre Pio was brutally beaten by Satan and his demons on numerous occasions. I have heard of others too. It was somewhat comforting knowing that I was not alone. I was beginning to think I was evil.

Please believe me, Satan does not have power and authority over me. GOD IS THE ONLY ONE WHO HAS POWER AND AUTHORITY OVER ME—PRAISE GOD! But you must understand that Satan really does exist. He usually works through other people or temptations.

My Spiritual Directors would always listen to what Satan would do and then direct me to do something more positive. The reason for this is if we dwell or obsess on Satan's nonsense, then we open our hearts and allow him to enter. All hell will rein on us then.

Spiritual Directors have told me that God allows Satan to attack us to keep us humble so that sin and pride does not occur. I heard that said about Padre Pio too. Padre Pio saw his Guardian Angel, Salvatore. Pio got mad at Salvatore one time because Satan was brutally beating him and Salvatore was standing there doing nothing. Pio was outraged until he understood why. Still he scolded Salvatore.

Delving into the demonic world is extremely frightening. I heard how individuals were virtually taken over by the demons and they never even realized what was happening to them. Many believed it was a gift from God, but it was not. Reading everything you can about spiritual warfare because of fascination is also extremely dangerous. One person told me that they wanted to know how Satan ticked. Please pray for him because he is not where he belongs. Opening yourself to the demonic world puts your soul in danger. Satan can come and just snatch it away without you being aware of it.

By the grace of God, He has given me the strength to stay focused on Him and not allow the evil one to distract me from God's Holy Will. Is it easy? No. But if you focus on the love of God, be firm in your devotion to God, trust explicitly in God, stay humble and steadfast, hang onto the cross, and desire to become closer and closer to God, then whatever temptations occur, they can be ignored or adverted. God only wants us to do our best. That is all God asks of us.

It was my intention to end this chapter here but I believe the

Blessed Mother wants me to go on so whoever reads this book will truly understand the power of the evil one. So in obedience and trust I will continue this chapter for Our Blessed Mother. Please do not obsess over these situations in which I am asked to share with you. When you open your heart or mind to evil, that is when evil will strike.

I am taking the following incidents out of my hand-written journals. All of my Spiritual Directors told me, "Linda, the experience you had is true, now let it go." I have done that for the most, but there are some that I am being reminded of. I have given these experiences over to the power and authority of God and know I am protected by the Blessed Mother.

One night, about four years ago, I was awoken by an evil force. When I looked toward the crucifix hanging on the wall in my bedroom, I saw a beautiful man standing there with blondish red hair. His eyes were as red as fire and trying to pierce my soul with fright. The Blessed Mother came and protected me. It was Satan. He looked at the crucifix, smiled, and disappeared.

One week later, I received a telephone call from a woman who had an abortion and needed to be counseled as soon as possible. I agreed to meet with her the next night because she sounded so desperate. On our first meeting she did all the talking. She began to speak about the father of her baby. On the wall behind the woman appeared the face of the blondish red haired man who appeared a week before in my bedroom. As she spoke the face became more enraged.

Not telling her what was taking place for fear of frightening her, I began to ask her questions pertaining to the father of the baby. She described him to me. She grew silent. I had a vision of this figure sitting in the chair next to us. I began to describe what I saw. She gasped and told me that was her boyfriend to the tee. She then told me the story of the incident after the abortion. They were in a hotel room and she began to feel an evil presence. When she looked into his eyes, they pierced her soul like fire. She tried to get away, but could not. She was paralyzed. As she spoke to me, she began to tremble and then a peace came over her. I knew our prayers were being answered and the transformation was beginning. God in all His love for her had taken a hold of her and Satan lost his fight. We both praised God for saving her. Of course, the relationship ended with the father of the baby and her new life began.

The thing that drives Satan crazy the most is when he loses a soul to God. Abortion is an abomination of the gift of life, which is God's gift to us. When a woman opens the door to encounter abortion, Satan steps in and begins his temptations of bringing to the mind of a woman negative thoughts such as; fear, confusion, and selfishness. Many have asked me throughout the past ten years of counseling, why women have abortions. My answer has always been because of fear, confusion, ignorance, and selfishness. It is not easy to choose abortion, but unless a woman has a positive influence in her life and a strong faith in God, she will fall for the deceptions of abortion.

Another young woman completed the S.A.V.E. program and began Spiritual Direction. She was sexually abused by her father and got into a satanic occult. She claimed to be gay and a professed witch. God revealed to me that she was not gay, she chose to be gay because of the horrendous life she had with sexual abuse and the relational problems with men. She stayed in contact with me during Spiritual Direction and asked me to attend a Healing Mass in which she was going to be prayed over. I attended to give her the love and support she needed.

The priest who was suppose to pray over her had an emergency and so he asked two of his healing team members to pray over her. After Mass the two members asked the young woman to join them in the confessional. She told them she would allow them to pray over her only if I could be present. I told the young woman I did not want to join them in the confessional, but the young woman insisted that she would not let this occur unless I was with her. Very apprehensively I agreed.

The young woman sat in a chair in the confessional. The two healing team members got down on their knees and I stood behind the young woman. The members began to pray. I put my hands on the young woman's shoulders for reassurance. After an hour of praying and speaking to the young woman, I began to smell something. The smell was nauseating, it burned my eyes, and made me sick to my stomach. The members were seeing things in the young woman's eyes. The horrible smell continued. As I looked up toward the door, a black figure appeared. It was a man standing in front of her. My heart began to pound as the members continued to pray even harder and louder.

Another hour passed and I saw another black figure of a woman holding onto the young woman. The members called her Jezebel, the young woman's imaginary friend that appeared during the time she was being sexually abused and during her occult activities. She befriended Jezebel and always believed Jezebel was her Guardian Angel.

The members gasped and I did not understand what was taking place. The odor was getting worse. I heard a voice tell me to wrap the young woman in a purple stole the priest wears for confession. I did so. Then the healing team member looked at me and said, "Linda, you will know when Jezebel is gone because the odor will be gone." "Oh great," I thought to myself. All I wanted to do was get out of the confessional. It was now the end of the third hour when I saw Jezebel flee and the room took on an odor of a beautiful rose garden. The members told us that the young woman's eyes were clear and sparkling.

The healing team members shared the experience with the priest the next day. When the Pastor of the Church found out what took place, he was so angry with all of us because we did not have his permission. I made sure I did not get involved in that kind of spiritual realm again. I have been woken up by demons who have appeared to me in many forms. Each has tried to frighten me by physical attacks, but my faith in God only grows stronger and my prayers are said that much harder. I belong to my Jesus, and I shall not surrender to evil.

I always go back to what every Spiritual Director ever told me, "Linda, you must be doing something right if demons are attacking you the way they are." Then I am comforted by St. Padre Pio.

You may be asking, "Why does God let this happen?" It is because of our pride which offends God so very much. Being attacked forces us to run for the Cross of Jesus Christ and cling to it as tight as we can. God never wants us to take our eyes off of the cross which is the gateway to heaven. We become easily distracted with worldly objects, but it is God that we should do everything we can to please Him for His Greater Glory. I learned this from St. Therese. Everything she did in a day, good or bad, she would offer it up to her bride, Jesus. EVERYTHING. It is the little things that she did that brought God so much pleasure. She too had attacks from Satan, but she turned to the Blessed Mother for refuge.

I am not implying that everything bad that happens in our life is from Satan. Remember, we have a free will and we must take responsibility for our actions. But I do believe that we are constantly tempted. It is up to us to hold tightly to the cross and stay focused on God's Will, not our will. God does not promise our life to be a bed of roses. He does promise that He will always love us unconditionally and be with us during the good times and the bad times if we only love and trust in Him.

If you want to get to heaven, you must be willing to suffer. Suffering is our salvation. Jesus suffered for you and me as He stretched out His arms on a tree and showed us how much He loved us by dying. If Jesus had to suffer, why are we any different?

Turn to God. Read the Bible and books on the Saints to understand how their lives changed by converting, surrendering, and abandoning their will to the Will of God. Believe me, it will help. It certainly helped me.

12

SEPARATION, LOSS, AND ABANDONMENT

This chapter is the most interesting part of my journey to God because it is a journey with my family and how they sacrificed everything in faith, to submit their lives to God's Holy Will.

When God asks us to separate and abandon ourselves from the world, we as human beings experience a sense of loss because we do not comprehend what that means. When God reveals His truth and light to us, we rejoice in His request. Separation and abandonment from the world means stripping every material thing from us that would distract us from loving God and desiring heaven.

In November 1998, while in deep prayer, I heard a voice tell me that I was in grave danger of attack and that I must prepare to leave Louisiana. When I heard this, my mind began to question if this voice was of God. I took the message into deep prayer and asked for three affirmations. In one day all three affirmations were received. Flabbergasted because this has never happened before, I went back into prayer and asked for three very unique affirmations that only God could hear in the depths of my heart and answer. In three days time all three affirmations were received. I shared the entire story with my husband. He took it to prayer, but in the interim believed that what I had heard was definitely coming from God.

It was Christmas time and the stores were all prepared for Christmas shopping. We grew up with lots of presents for Christmas. It was a tradition that was carried through generation after generation. So when I heard in prayer, "STRIP!," of course there was great difficulty dealing with what it meant. Now you have to understand, I was a person who had three closets full of clothing and shoes to match every outfit. Friends called me "Imelda Marcos." When God tells someone to strip, He wants all the material objects that have caused sin and distraction out of the person's life. Clothing and shoes were definitely a sin and distraction for me. I could not go in the mall without buying something. I was confessing it all the time. A compulsive shopper was the new psychiatric term being used that described me perfectly. So when I was told to keep enough clothing for two weeks and flat shoes, well, upset was my reaction.

"STRIP," kept going over and over in my mind. Finally, out of trying to be obedient, I went through the closets. I started with clothing that was just a little too snug. That took one black plastic bag. "I can do this," I said to myself as I gritted my teeth. God knew this task was not going to be easy for me. Then the clothes I did not like any more filled the second black plastic bag. By then the shame of the sin of gluttony was hitting me smack in the face. A total of twenty black plastic thirty-two gallon bags were filled with clothing and shoes. When I looked in the closet, what God had requested of me was the only things hanging there. I was shocked and amazed.

I called Jacqualine and shared the story with her and she could not believe her ears. It worked out that her daughter, Michelle, was the same size as me and took everything. Michelle was like a little child, she was so excited. I praised God that He brought Michelle into my life because she is so beautiful inside and out and it gave me peace knowing that God chose her to receive these items.

When my family heard what I was doing this, they joined in and so their clothing was also given to those God chose. We were all feeling very peaceful. Then it was time to strip the house of the excess pictures and nicknacks. We did that also and God had chosen people for those items too.

Once everything was stripped down as far as we could go, it was Christmas. For the first time in our lives, we had a Christmas with Jesus. We gave each other one gift instead of the fifteen. The gift was to be religious and something that would touch the hearts of each of us. The Christmas tree was a small artificial table top type. Humble! Every year it was a real eight foot blue spruce tree with beautiful decorations. We really began to experience the true meaning of Jesus' birth. We went to Midnight Mass, which was absolutely beautiful. After Mass, we came home, turned on Christmas music, and opened our gifts. It was awesome!

After Christmas I heard in prayer that it was time to move on and leave Louisiana for Kentucky. Erlanger, Kentucky to be exact. ERLANGER, KENTUCKY, ARE YOU KIDDING?????? The voice sounded like Padre Pio. All of a sudden the bedroom filled with a strong incense smell of sweet tobacco and roses. Before me stood Padre Pio. Shocked and dismayed, again I said, "Erlanger, Kentucky, are you kidding?" "NO," he said. "God needs you there. You are in danger here and you must leave as soon as possible," he reiterated.

Back to prayer I went. More affirmations were requested and the answers were once again immediate. A family meeting was required again. Since we were operating on a fixed income, one of the affirmations was that if it was the Will of God that we move, then He must send the money. The family prayed and asked for affirmations. Immediately they received theirs. Mom and Jim decided to travel to Kentucky by plane, rent a car and hotel, and set up an appointment with a Realtor. Three days after the family meeting, the money came to cover the entire cost of the trip and then some. We wrote a note around the neck of Jim's statue of St. Joseph entrusting in his intercession.

The trip was arranged and Jim and Mom flew to Kentucky. The first Realtor did not work out. The Realtor told them he did not have time for them and just drove them around. Two days before they were ready to return to Louisiana, a house had not been found. Jim and Mom were concerned. In prayer, Sharon and I had received that they needed to visit a convent in Walton, just outside of the Erlanger area, to see what it was like.

Mother Ellen, the Superior for St. Joseph the Worker Convent in Walton, invited Jim and Mom in to talk and have some tea. Two hours later they were still talking to Mother, so she invited Jim and Mom to join her and the sisters for Benediction and prayer. They agreed. Mom and Jim entrusted the trip and move to the intercession of St. Joseph because they did not know what to do.

After Benediction and prayer had concluded, Mother directed Jim and Mom to their maintenance man for help. The maintenance man directed them to the Realtor down the street. In total peace and faith, Jim and Mom went to the Realtor. In one hour, the Realtor had thirty properties lined up. Jim decided to stay an extra two days and rearranged their trip. The Realtor had twenty properties set up each day. Meanwhile, we were pre-approved for a home loan that was for much more money then our present home in Slidell. We were shocked. Finally, a house was found and our proposal was made. As soon as Jim and Mom walked into the house, they knew that it was the one. The only problem that we could foresee was that there was two other contracts on the same house, but we continued to believe that this house was the one.

Jim and Mom returned home totally exhausted. We believed that St. Joseph interceded, the Blessed Mother removed all the road blocks, and God's Will was in motion. We were at peace.

Back in Louisiana the chaos continued, but we never lost the belief that this move was God's Will. We went to two different reality companies before we were satisfied. Our home went up for sale on March 2, 1999. We believed it would sell immediately because we invested so much work in it, especially the vinyl siding. On May 8, 1999, a buyer put a contract on our home. People were telling me Satan was trying to force us out of Slidell, but I never shared with anyone the real importance of us leaving. I spoke to three priests, who told me they believed our move was from God, even though they were shocked that the move was happening so quickly. Once you say "YES" to God and accept His Will, things move very quickly. The priests were very disappointed that we were leaving because of our ties to the community and the S.A.V.E. healing ministry. But they all said that God sends people where He needs them the most.

Remember, when you do the Will of God, Satan will try to stick his nose into it and fill you with doubt and confusion, which he is so good at doing. The house in Kentucky that we had a proposal on fell through. The man of the house died and the house went into probate. This concerned us because we did not have the money to make another trip. The Realtor and I played buy a house using fax machines. It did not work. Another family meeting and back to deep prayer. The money was sent and back to Kentucky we went. This time it was Jim and I, which God gave me the strength to do.

Two days we looked for a house, nothing. We went to St. Joseph's Church in Cold Springs, which is right outside of Erlanger. We were told that the Blessed Mother had been appearing to a woman there, but since the crowds had grown so big, they moved to another location. When we entered St. Joseph's Church, we could feel the power and strength of the Holy Family. The statue of the Blessed Mother was the same one as the Medjugore statue. Jim and I lit a candle, held hands, and prayed in front of the Blessed Mother statue. Her face became alive and she directed us to pray in front of St. Joseph, so we did. We returned to Our Blessed Mother and sat before her. She gifted Jim and I with an overwhelming peace. We knew we belonged in Kentucky and the Holy Family was going to direct us to the house God chose for us.

It seemed like we had looked at 150 homes. We were exhausted, but we moved on. I had a sense to call the mortgage company to see the highest amount of money we could be approved for. When we were told, it blew our minds. So we pressed on by looking at another category of homes. Three times we were brought to a small community in a place called Crittenden. Crittenden is considered country with horses, cows, and farm land. I did not like the community, but God has a sense of humor because once we were upgraded in price, the first home we looked at was in the community I did not like. We were told to look for a small humble home. We found it. We needed a ranch home where everything was on one floor. In Kentucky, they have basements that are usually finished. The basement is used for a familyroom, bathroom and extra bedrooms.

My first reaction to the house was, "NO WAY." Humble and small it was, and it was everything that the Holy Family described to us. Then we walked in the back yard. I thought I was in Medjugore, a mini Medjugore. The backyard had rolling hills, trees, butterflies, birds, and totally peaceful. Jim and I looked at one another and knew this was it. When we put a proposal on the house, it was accepted. Our house in Slidell was already sold and we had to leave the premises on June 9, 1999, but we did not know where we were going to stay until we closed on the Kentucky home. The owner of the Kentucky house told us to move into the house rent free until closing. Jim and I looked at each other and could not believe what we were hearing, but we were praising God and the Holy Family. We signed all the necessary papers and returned to Slidell.

On June 9, 1999, we went to the closing for the Slidell house. We thought all of our things would fit in one twenty-four-foot Ryder truck, but Mom and Sharon had to rent a fifteen-foot Ryder truck for their belongings. Jim drove our truck and Sharon drove her truck with her cat. Mom, the dog, and I drove in my car. Between traffic, getting ill, getting a flat on the towing ramp which was attached to the truck Jim was driving and towing his Jeep, and losing each other, the trip was memorable. We had no idea Kentucky was so far from Louisiana.

The Realtor and his family helped us move into the Kentucky house. We unloaded both trucks in one day. The house was unbelievable and we all sat down and laughed and kept praising God. When I walked into the house this time, I fell in love with it and it looked different to me. The things I disliked about it were acceptable. It was awesome! The peace was indescribable and all I could do was stand on the deck in the back yard and stare at the mini Medjugore and thank God for it all. When God told me that the door He was opening was going to be far greater than the one He was closing, He was really serious. I knew He had a reason for us moving here to this home. We are in the heart of Baptist country. EVANGELIZE!!!!

Now that we have lived in the house for three months, Sharon and I love it. Mom and Jim are still adjusting. The dog and cat love it here too. It is ironic, everyone was worried that the dog and cat would not get along at all. Surprise! The dog and cat love each other and get along extremely well. God is good.

So when you hear the voice of God say, "STRIP," or when you hear Him say, "MOVE," and you pray, discern, affirm, and speak to your family and priests, and all the signs affirm what God is telling you, DO AS GOD HAS ASKED BECAUSE OUT OF OBEDIENCE, LOVE, TRUST, AND FAITH—COMES GOD'S MISSION OF NEED. And isn't that what life is about—pleasing God?

I do not miss the state of Louisiana or Slidell. I do miss my buddy, Jacqualine, and the priests who were so instrumental in my life. We stay in contact with letters and telephone calls. I miss my adopted sister, Judy, who became a Carmelite Nun. Her Carmelite name is Sister Teresa Benedicta, Of the Holy Wounds. We are so proud of her. We have adopted the Carmelite Convent in Lafayette and they have adopted us. It is wonderful and we are blessed. Sister Teresa was an inspiration for me. When she joined Carmel as they call it, she had to relinquish everything of the world to become the bride of Jesus. Was it easy for her? "NO." But she did it for the love of God. Many people who despised her and persecuted her prayed that she would fail at Carmel. But God is mightier and stronger than those who tried to destroy her. He sent her to a loving environment with Carmelite Nuns who are humble, holy, and wonderful women. Sr. Teresa Benedicta, who was named after St. Edith Stein, is and will always be a blessing to our family.

Once God gifts and graces you with the touch of heaven through a dream, vision, His presence or the presence of a heavenly being, your desire for the world will diminish and your focus will be on heaven and heaven only. Faith plays an enormous role in God's Will for our life. Faith in God can move mountains. Faith in God can change a hardened heart into one that is strong and filled with love—the love of God. Faith in God can help you to accept the daily trials of life knowing that God will gift you with the strength and courage to endure them. God is with you always, comforting and embracing you in your time of need. We are never alone.

Abandonment of the world is total faith in God. As we journey through life—through our peaks and valleys—through our joys and sorrows—through our pains and sufferings, God, in all His unconditional love, is with us. What an awesome truth!

God who loved me in all my mess-ups, was there to pick me up, comfort me, and love me unconditionally. No one in my life has ever done that for me. In all I have done, in all the hurt and pain I have caused God, He still loves me so much not to leave me where I am, but to help me grow closer and closer to Him. He wants me to keep moving down the narrow path that leads to His loving arms—the final destination—heaven. Then I can be with Him for all eternity. That is what I want so desperately, to be in the

Presence of God forever. Nothing in this world matters more to me than that. Being with God is the ultimate desire. That is why when God told me to abandon from the world, I surrendered. When God told me to strip, I surrendered. When God asked me to suffer for Him, I surrendered. These were the gifts I gave to God out of total love, praise, and thankfulness. What amazed me so much was that I abandoned, separated, and lost all for the love of God and I would do it all again if He asked me. These actions were done in humble obedience and I do not regret my actions or choose to look back at all, nor am I being prideful.

Out of this journey God has blessed me with one powerful vision which I hold to the depths of my heart. I would like to share it with you. The vision was a gift from God when my suffering and the desolation of my soul was so intense that I was just trying to hold onto the light. This is not a self-serving vision either. Some call this experience the dark night of the soul, while others call it the desert. All I know is that I experienced a deep dark hole that I could not climb out of. I struggled and prayed, but in God's love, He gave me a gift to cling to—this vision—and that is why I am led to share it with you so those who have experienced the same thing can cling to this with hope.

The vision was: I am taken to the Throne of God in heaven on the wings of the Holy Spirit. When we arrive, Jesus, the Blessed Mother, St. Michael the Archangel, St. Therese of Lisieux, St. Francis of Assisi, and St. Pio are standing there waiting for me. Jesus and the Blessed Mother dress me in the most beautiful bridal gown.

As a gift to God, I place my heart on a golden tray which St. Michael is carrying. The Saints hug me and kiss me. Padre Pio says to me, "Welcome to the family." As I look down, there is Cecilia, Gabriel, and Sarah, my children in heaven, tugging at my gown with a long train attached. The three of them give me all kinds of loving. As I look up, there are my Holy Guardian Angels, Michael, Peter, Paul, and Tobias. We embrace.

Then the procession begins up, what appears to be fifty steps, to the Throne of God. There is a chair to the left of God and a chair to the right of God. The Blessed Mother takes my left arm and

Jesus takes my right arm as we process up the stairs to God. Everyone mentioned is in front of us except my babies who are carrying the train to the gown.

As we arrive at the top of the Throne of God, standing before me is God the Father radiating so much love, that it is undescribable. Jesus and Mary present me to Him. He takes me into Him arms and holds me for a period of time while telling me how much He loves me.

Choirs of Angels are singing magnificently. God and I look at each other and He puts His heart in my chest as a gift. The love we have for one another is beyond all words, in fact, it would make you speechless. We kiss and I totally and completely surrender all that I am to Him. We embrace again and exchange the words, "I love you." Jesus sits to the right of God and I sit to the left of God until He crowns me as His bride forever.

So when I am asked how can I do what I do, it is for this reason. With total humility, I love God the Father so much that I would do anything for Him, even suffer and die for Him. I believe that this magnificent vision is the ultimate destination for me and everyone who submits to the love of God, but we must suffer tremendously, sacrifice, and save as many souls as we can all for the love and glory of God and our salvation. We can not get to heaven without penance, suffering, sacrificing, praying, and saving souls for the love and glory of God. We must do it all with joy in our hearts. ALL FOR THE GLORY OF GOD. AMEN.

13

THE TRIUMPH OF THE IMMACULATE HEART

So much I have learned has come from the education Monsignor Richard Carroll has taught we, his children. Our Blessed Mother had Monsignor Carroll prepare his children for the Triumph of the Immaculate Heart. I am humbled by this priest and know that what he has prepared us for, we must now go out and evangelize to others. We are living in exciting times.

The Triumph of the Immaculate Heart has been spoken about in so many ways. Some try to put the fear of God in us by telling us of the horrible things that will occur if we do not come back to God and change our lives. Even though much that has been written is true, as we journey closer to the millennium, we must try to understand that this world must be purified before we destroy it ourselves. It has been reported that people are coming back to Church in droves to prepare for what is coming.

We should have the fear of God, even though God is a loving, merciful, and forgiving God. He especially radiates a love that no human being can ever imitate or comprehend. It is an unconditional love of forgiveness that no human being can master or manifest. God loves us no matter what.

But we are living in times when many in the world live for the world. Materialism. power, pride, arrogance, and selfishness is the way of life. We have taken God for granted. Our cup is overflowing with hatred and sin, and now the just God must intervene. The just God will allow things to occur to bring this world back to their scenes or even their knees. His mercy endures forever, but now is the time of justice. We, as a world, have no one to blame but ourselves if the hand of God falls. We must atone for our sinfulness. ONLY GOD KNOWS WHEN THE TIME WILL COME WHEN HIS HAND WILL FALL AND THE WORLD WILL ATONE FOR THEIR SINFULNESS.

Many authors, prophets, and visionaries have been gifted with part of the puzzle, but only God knows all of the puzzle. That is why we turn to the Holy Father, Pope John Paul II. He is a man of enormous love of God and of Our Blessed Mother. We must look to him for direction. Many false prophets, false visionaries and others who want to use scare tactics of lies and deception will rise up and cause chaos, confusion, and division amongst the different religions.

The Holy Father directs us to do the simple requests that come directly from the Blessed Mother and heaven which are: have faith in God's love for us, pray the rosary daily which is the most powerful tool of prayer and can deter most, if not all of the Chastisements from occurring. Attend Mass every day, especially Sundays and the Holy days. Do the Five first Saturdays for the graces of being saved from the fires of hell and for yourself and your families to be protected by the Immaculate Heart of Mary. Wear a scapular. Go to confession at least once a month, if not more regularly, to cleanse your soul and have a pure heart. But most of all do all these things with a joyful heart for the glory of God. By doing these things you have nothing to fear and you and your family will be protected by the Immaculate Heart of Mary. It is a promise that Our Lady made to all of us.

While you do the First Five Saturdays, consecrate yourself to the Immaculate Heart of Mary using the book called, "Preparation for Total Consecration According to St. Louis Marie de Montfort." This tool is one of the most powerful tools of protection during these times of trials. She will not let any harm come to you or your family if you put your trust in the Immaculate Heart of Mary.

I believe that the world must atone for all of the babies who have been aborted. The shedding of the blood of the innocence has brought so much sadness and sorrow to Jesus' and Mary's Hearts. These baby martyrs cry out to God for justice because their lives were snuffed away because of ignorance, fear, and selfishness. An unborn child is a baby from conception. So much blood has been poured over this world with over 35 million babies killed since 1971. 1.5 million babies are killed each year. I believe and it is my own belief, that even those who have not had an abortion experience will still have to answer for this horrendous act of violence. Seventeen people are effected by one abortion. SEVENTEEN!!!

That is not including those who do not want to get involved in the abortion issue or continue to stay totally ignorant. ABORTION IS THE KILLING OF A HUMAN LIFE.

A visionary from Medjugore was reported to ask Our Blessed Mother during an apparition why the AIDS virus has not been cured. Her response was because the child who was chosen to find the cure was aborted. Think about how many aborted children may have found the cure for cancer and other incurable diseases.

We can only find solace from the world through the Immaculate Heart of Mary. She is coming in all her glory to reign in peace for the world. It is reported that the Triumph of the Immaculate Heart will occur before or during the year 2,000. Once again, only God knows when this will occur, but Our Blessed Mother promises refuge to those who have consecrated to her Immaculate Heart. She will protect those from a pagan society which has denied God in order to build idols of pleasure and money, of pride and egoism, and of amusement and impurity. But it does not matter whether you are Roman Catholic, Baptist, Lutheran, Methodist, Buddhist, or another religion, the Blessed Mother is your mother. She is the mother of the entire world because she is the mother of Jesus Christ, who is our brother.

Many faiths only acknowledge Mary as conceiving Jesus, and there is controversy about the manner in which Jesus was conceived. So I am going to share God's truth and light on the issue. Mary, a fifteen-year-old young women was born pure, sinless, and specifically chosen by God to conceive His Son, Jesus Christ. Contemplate this openly and honestly.

We know Jesus is God, the part of the Holy Trinity, and totally pure. Why would God choose a woman who was a sinner to conceive His Son? That does not make sense to me. Jesus had to be conceived by a woman who was purified by God at conception.

Mary, a young single woman, had the Archangel Gabriel, a messenger from God, come to her and announce that she had been specifically chosen by God to have His Son. The Angel continued by telling Mary that God's Holy Spirit would come upon her and she would conceive the Son of God. God, who is the Creator of life, chose Mary to be the Mother of His Son, Jesus, and chose His Holy Spirit to be Mary's Well Beloved Spouse. If we proclaim that all things are possible with God, then why do we question God's truth and light?

God chooses all kinds of people to do His Will, to be His hands, His feet, and even allows His thoughts to be manifested into a chosen one through the power of His Holy Spirit. God speaks to our hearts, if we only listen.

I am an instrument of God's love and mercy. God calls me "Jesus' sorrow." He took me, a grave sinner with a high school diploma and forgave me for the horrendous sins I committed. He loved me unconditionally and blessed me with the power of His Holy Spirit. I was introduced to Jesus by His Mother, Mary. And God asked me to reach out to those individuals who were brokenhearted and suffering from an abortion experience by gifting me with the S.A.V.E. Roman Catholic Healing Program. The Holy Spirit gave me the knowledge to write the S.A.V.E. Roman Catholic Healing Manuals for Women, Men, Grandparents to the Unborn, Family Members and Friends, and this book.

I have had no formal education in writing, except in what I learned in high school, nor do I hold any educational degrees, which has always unbalanced the well educated. God took my experiences and asked me to write so others could be set free by embracing God's love and mercy.

If not for the Blessed Mother and her intercession to Jesus, I would never have met the Father in the manner in which I did. His love is beyond all love. No human being on the face of this earth can love you as much as God does. It is the most awesome love you can ever experience and I thank Jesus and Mary for their intercession. When the Triumph of the Immaculate Heart occurs, everyone all over the world will finally understand that the Mother of Jesus, Mary, in all her glory was chosen by God the Father to reign as Queen of heaven and earth. Then all faiths will join as one and honor her as she for so long has deserved. The truth and light will then set each person free.

Let this humanity return, like the prodigal son, into the arms of the Heavenly Father, who awaits all with love, so that a new, profound and universal reconciliation may be thus achieved between God and humanity. Amen.

14

THE FINAL BATTLE; DEATH AND HEAVEN

We are born to live and to die. Life is a gift from God. Death is the ultimate price we pay for our sinfulness. God knew us before our parents or even before we were thought about. Even before our conception, God knew us. We have a time to be born and a time to die. All chosen by God.

We hear of people who fear death because of the unknown. There are people who want to die in their sleep, a quick death with no pain or suffering. I have never heard anyone say, "I want to suffer from an excruciating disease, like cancer, and during my suffering I will lift each moment up to save souls from damnation all for the love and glory of God." When I contemplate this comment, I find joy and peace in my heart.

In the suffering I have done in the past three years, I have tried to live by that comment. I remember when I would contemplate death and tell God what a chicken I was over pain and suffering and to please take me quick in my sleep. Thinking back on those times, I now chuckle because of the understanding of what suffering really means.

Suffering for others, especially when God personally asks you, means that souls that were going to be lost forever in the depths of hell, may now have the opportunity of being saved. What an awesome responsibility! The greatest sufferer and soul saver was Jesus Christ. Jesus became tremendously saddened when He lost a soul.

An example of a lost soul would be Judas. Judas was filled with lust, power, arrogance, and greed. He sold Jesus for money. Even up to the time of the event in the Garden of Gethsemane when Judas turned Jesus over to the Sanhedrin to be put to death, Jesus still tried to help Judas see the truth to his evil ways so he would be converted and saved. But Judas' heart was so hardened that he would not listen to Jesus. Jesus wants everyone saved. That is why He preached so much on the love of God, forgiveness, prayer, reconciliation, purity, and poverty.

Today, we hear about Padre Pio, who suffered the five wounds of Jesus (the stigmata), and suffered to save the souls in purgatory, especially those who had no one to pray to them. Padre Pio called them Holy Souls. We are taught in the Roman Catholic faith that purgatory is a place of purification when we die. It sits between heaven and hell and is reported to have many levels.

Visionaries from Medjugorje and around the world describe purgatory as a place of intense heat or fire. Unlike hell, purgatory does not torment a soul with unspeakable hatred for eternity. In purgatory a soul is tormented by the desire of heaven. The way we live our life and the sins we have committed, depends on how long we are in purgatory.

In heaven, time does not exist as we know it. A minute on earth could be eternity in heaven. The same goes for purgatory.

There are many levels of purgatory as stated earlier. A visionary from Medjugorje reported that purgatory is a place of fire, but not eternal fire like hell. The fire that engulfs the soul in purgatory is to purify the soul of its sin. The way we live on earth and the sins we die with must be atoned and purified before we are embraced by heaven.

While attending the St. Ignatius Exercises at St. Margaret Mary, we had topics to meditate on that helped us to deepen our spiritual journey with God. I remember the topic I was reading and visualizing on the Birth of Jesus. I saw myself as one of the shepherds. An angel appeared to us and told us to go to Bethlehem that a child has been born who will save the Jewish people. When we arrived, Mary and Joseph were with the baby Jesus. Mary stood before me and asked me if I wanted to hold the baby Jesus. I said, "Yes." She put Him in my arms and I was overwhelmed with so much love, peace, and joy.

Then there was another experience when I saw myself following the steps of Calvary with Jesus, Mary, his mother, and Mary Magdalen. At the Crucifixion, looking up at Jesus hanging on the cross, dying for my sins and the sins of the world and the persecution of those who stood around staring at Him, I remember it was the most gut wrenching experience I ever had. The scriptures came alive to me. It is God's Will that we experience such a grace.

I have previously shared with you the experience of my three desires of death; heaven, purgatory, and hell in chapter nine. I do not think most people really understand what sin does to our souls. The soul is stained with ugliness. I know that if I had died after my abortions with living a promiscuous lifestyle as I did, I believe I would have ended up in hell.

This reminds me of the reported story that Maria, one of the visionaries from Medjugorje, told a group of people. When the Blessed Mother took Maria to visit hell, Maria saw an absolutely gorgeous blonde young woman enter the fire of hell and come out of the fire as a horrible looking creature. She was horrified.

Maria asked the Blessed Mother why this happened to the beautiful young woman. The Blessed Mother told her it was because her life was centered on lust and impure sex, instead of God. It made me stop to think how very important the relationship with God is and the Sacrament of Reconciliation. The Lord has told us that the road to heaven is very narrow.

This is the hour of the final battle; it is therefore also the hour of the victory of the Immaculate Heart of Mary. Let us pray together, loving and invoking the Holy Spirit, whom the Father will give you in superabundance through the Son, that you may soon see new heavens and a new earth.

Let us also begin today to take our Roman Catholic faith much more serious since we do not know the hour when God will call us home. When we stand before Him in judgement and He asks us, "Why should I let you in heaven?" what will you respond?

In His Truth and In His Light

15

A JOURNEY TO THE TRUE PRESENCE OF GOD

In Monsignor Richard L. Carroll's book, "The Third Millennium; The Triumph of Our Lady" he reports that, "the lack of belief and faith in the True Presence of Jesus Christ in the Holy Eucharist brought the division of the Roman Catholic Church. A Protestant Reformation began. The drop in Mass attendance went from 97% in 1960 to 30% presently, people do not attend Sunday Mass and if they do, many receive Jesus in mortal sin, only a few of the faithful go to confession on a regular basis, and there are those who do not believe that the Blessed Mother was chosen specifically by God, a virgin, to conceive the Son of God, Jesus, sinless. They cannot accept the Immaculate Conception so they choose to sin because they feel they are also free of sin."

The True Presence of God is not being adored, honored, revered, and loved as He should. Pope John Paul II has reported that the year 2,000 will be Eucharistic. This means that the Roman Catholic Church will be reunited by the power of the Holy Spirit, hearts will be changed, and many conversions will take place. The True Presence of God will once again be adored and looked upon as Jesus' Body, Blood, Soul, and Divinity, and peace will fall upon the world. Our Blessed Mother tells us that every tabernacle on earth will have her presence along with the Holy Angels as the Choirs sing songs of adoration. Jesus will reign again in the hearts of the world and the miracle of love will be boundless for all our brothers and sisters.

Jesus will come alive in the Eucharist and renew the faith of those who embrace Him with love, belief, and surrender. The chosen will be the lights for the rest of the world, and examples of God's truth and light that Jesus is really present in the Eucharist. Reparation to the world will occur everywhere.

Jesus' reign will occur at the same time as the miracle of the

True Presence of Jesus in the Eucharist in releasing His love and transforming the Roman Catholic Church and all humanity. The Roman Catholic Churches throughout the world who have honored and adored the True Presence of God with twenty-four hour Eucharistic Adoration or some form of Adoration, will experience the true power of love from God. Countless healings and conversions have been reported by individuals who faithfully showed honor and respect to Jesus in Eucharistic Adoration.

We incorporated visits to Eucharistic Adoration in the S.A.V.E. (Suffering Abortion Victims Embraced) Healing Programs. The women reported tremendous peace, love, and mystical visions. The men reported peace and understanding. The women found Jesus there with His arms opened inviting them into His loving embrace. Their hearts were healed and converted and their personal relationship with Jesus was miraculously deepened and changed forever. A few reported that they saw their children standing on the altar or their child's face in the Eucharistic Host in the Monstrance on the altar. Some heard Jesus' voice in the depths of their hearts, speaking words of love, forgiveness, peace, healing, and wholeness.

Since naming the unborn children is a part of the preparation for the Memorial Mass said in their honor, many women have reported hearing their baby's name being chosen by God and given to them in prayer prior to the Memorial Mass while sitting in front of the Eucharistic Jesus.

A friend shared with me about an experience of a woman who was kneeling down praying in front of the Eucharistic Jesus and she had a vision of the Crucified Jesus bleeding in the Eucharistic Host. We hear about Eucharistic miracles that occur all over the world. The Eucharistic Host turns to flesh and begins to bleed real blood. You can not tell me that Jesus is not telling us that He is alive! I know Jesus is alive in the Eucharist. Everytime we receive Jesus during the communion of the Holy Mass, we receive Jesus' Body, Blood, Soul, and Divinity. To disbelieve this truth is sacrilege, which is a grave and mortal sin. By not believing this truth, you are insulting Jesus and betraying Jesus. Remember, Jesus was slaughtered on a tree for you and me. He opened His arms as far as they could go to show His love for us as He was nailed to that tree.

All, so we would be saved. If that is not true unconditional love, I do not know what is?

During the Consecration of every Holy Mass throughout the world, Jesus gives Himself as a sacrifice by coming down from heaven and shedding His Precious Body and Blood for us out of love. Why do people show Him such ingratitude and arrogance?

The Eucharist should be the center of your prayer and of your life. I believe that people choose not to believe in the Eucharistic Jesus because Jesus may request them to do something which they are not willing to do. All Jesus requests is that we love Him with our whole heart and whole soul by sacrificing something that is important to us for Him, like Him for us. Even though we have free wills, Jesus requests that we always do the Will of His Father.

In my life I have said "no" to God so many times, which I regret to this day. When the path got too unbearable, I dropped down on my knees and surrendered to God. Through the power of the Holy Spirit, He showed me that even though I would have to suffer by doing God's Will, it was much better than if I chose to do my own will. Now I look at saying "no" to God as literally slapping Him across the face because of all He has done for me and given me. I know that it was not God punishing me by my rebellion of Him or by my arrogance, pride, and selfishness, it was me punishing myself.

I invite you, as Jesus and Mary always do, to visit an Eucharistic Adoration Chapel. Take nothing but yourself. Sit before the Eucharistic Jesus and tell Him everything that is bottled up inside of you by releasing all your hurt and pain that is now piercing your soul. Cry if you are led to. Hold nothing back. Tears are a sign that the Holy Spirit is beginning the healing process. After you are finished speaking to Jesus, sit silently and close your eyes. Allow Jesus into your heart so He can administer to you as He deems necessary. Remain with Jesus without looking at the time on your wrist watch. Just allow yourself to be engulfed in the most amazing love relationship you have ever experienced in your entire life.

I was told a story once about an old man. The man would come into a Church everyday and sit down. The priest watched the man for a long time. All the man would do was come into the Church, sit down, and stare. Finally, the priest was curious, so he walked over to the old man and said, "I have noticed for a long time you come here and you walk in, you sit down, and you stare. I would like to know what you are doing?" The old man looked at the young priest and said, "I look at Him (Jesus) and He (Jesus) looks at me." In the old man's silence and faith he met Jesus and their relationship and love for each other was unconditional. This is how we need to go before the Eucharistic Jesus, so He too can love us and nurture us by speaking to us in truth and light and healing our hurts and pains.

Prostate yourself before the Eucharistic Jesus. Just lay down on the floor with your arms stretched out in total humble adoration. Make reparation of His sufferings. Pray that the trials the world is now facing will be shortened and that the new era of peace will flow in like a breath of fresh, pure, heavenly fragrant air. Watch how your life will change and be transformed like never before in your life.

Let the truth and light of God penetrate your very heart, mind, body, and soul by His embracing love. Then you will be able to humbly and honestly say, "I believe in the True Presence of God."

16

THE FINAL CHAPTER

I believe Our Blessed Mother is asking me to end this book with a message from the Marian Movement of Priests book called "To The Priests—Our Lady's Beloved Sons." This book is a collective writing of messages by Father Don Stefano Gobbi, a priest from Italy, who received interior messages from Our Blessed Mother from July 7, 1973 to December 31, 1997.

These messages are invitations to priests, to religious, and to lay persons preparing us all—the entire world, for the Triumph of the Immaculate Heart. As Our Blessed Mother speaks to Father Gobbi, the truth and light of warnings, of invitations, of preparations, and definitely of her undying love for her children, is conveyed so simply and humbly.

I highly recommend that you purchase a copy of these writings for your personal reading and to share with your family and friends. You may even consider beginning a Cenacle Prayer Group, which Our Blessed Mother requested Father Gobbi to establish Cenacles of Prayer throughout the world. Call the Marian Movement of Priests at (207)-398-3375, for a copy of the book and information on how to begin a Cenacle Prayer Group.

In this time of uncertainty, this book will help you to understand what is being foretold by Our Blessed Mother in her own words. In prayer Our Blessed Mother gave me #396—Mother of Intercession and of Reparation. Father Gobbi received this message on December 31, 1988 in Como, Italy. The message reads as follows;

"Gather together in prayer with Me, beloved children, at the end of this year which has been particularly dedicated to me. I am your heavenly Mother. I am the Mother of Intercession and of Reparation.

—My maternal task is that of interceding each day for you, before my Son, Jesus. As an attentive and concerned Mother, I am asking for all the graces that you have need of in order to walk along the road of goodness, of love and of holiness.

For my sinful children, I obtain the grace of repentance, of a change of heart, of return to the Lord. For my sick children, I grant the grace of understanding the meaning of every suffering, of accepting it with docility, of offering it with love, of carrying one's own cross with trust and with filial obedience to the Will of the Lord. For my good children, I obtain the gift of perseverance in good. For my priest-sons, I intercede that they may be holy ministers and faithful to Jesus and to his Gospel.

Each new day that opens out corresponds to a new act of prayer on the part of your heavenly Mother, to help you to walk forward, in the desert of your time, along the road of love and of the faithful fulfillment of the Will of God, which must be accomplished by you with filial docility.

—My maternal task is also that of offering reparation for the great evil which, still today, is being committed in the world. I unite myself with each Holy Mass which is celebrated, to offer to the Heavenly Father the precious blood of his Son, Jesus, who is still immolating and sacrificing Himself for you on every altar of the earth. It is only his divine blood, shed for you, that can wash away all the evil, the sin, the hatred, the impurity, the iniquity that covers the world. Thus, in a spirit of maternal reparation, I unite to the blood of Christ all the sufferings which I gather together, each day, along your pathway.

I unite to the blood of Jesus, the blood poured out by millions of babies still being killed in their mother's wombs and of all the victims of hatred, of violence and of wars.

I unite to the blood of Jesus, all the sufferings of the sick, especially those who are stricken with grave, humiliating and incurable maladies.

I unite to the blood of Jesus, the agonies of the dying, the sufferings of the poor, of the marginalized, of the little, of the exploited, of the persecuted. I unite to the blood of Jesus, each suffering of the good, of those consecrated, of the priests.

I unite to the blood of Jesus, the great cross which the Church must carry today for the salvation of all humanity.

At the close of this year, which has been particularly entrusted to me, I want to associate you also in my maternal task of interceding and of making reparation for all my children.

And even so, in the darkness and the coldness which still surrounds the world, I urge you to live in hope and in great trust, because I am ever praying and making reparation in order to obtain, for all, new days of peace and salvation."

Our Blessed Mother continues to reassure us of her undying love for us and that she is with us always, interceding for us and making reparation for us in our time of need. It is through Our Blessed Mother that we find her Son, Jesus, and it is through Jesus, that we find God the Father.

This year, 1999, is the year of God the Father. Jacqualine mailed me a book called, "God The Father—Consecration and Feast Day For THE FATHER OF ALL MANKIND," written by The Father of All Mankind Apostolate, (412)-788-4530. Jacqualine is still a member of St. Margaret Mary Church in Slidell and the entire parish took part in the eight solemn days using the book. I found the eight days to be an unbelievable journey with God. I began the journey with confession and Sunday Mass and ended the eight days the same way. During the eight days, God revealed many things to me, especially seeing myself through God's eyes. What a humbling experience that deepened our relationship even more. It was awesome!

The book explains, "its greatest significance in these times is that it provides us with an opportunity, (1) to honor God Our Father, (2) to offer Him our "fiat," and (3) to consecrate ourselves to Him. In this way, we are truly cooperating with our Mother Mary in the Triumph of Her Immaculate Heart. We are returning to our Father, we are offering Him our unconditional "fiat" as Mary and Jesus did; and we are consecrating ourselves to Him—totally. As He so richly deserves, we are finally knowing, loving, serving, and honoring Him as God Our Father—The Father of All Mankind."

Call this Apostolate for what is needed to consecrate yourself and your family to God the Father. Our Blessed Mother invites you to do so. You will be glad you did. It will definitely enhance your relationship with God.

I would also like to share with you Monsignor Richard L.

Carroll's new book, "Finding God the Father," found in your local bookstores. Monsignor Carroll not only was my Pastor when I lived in Slidell, he is also my Spiritual Father. I love him very much and have valued his knowledge on the Blessed Mother and the Triumph of the Immaculate Heart, the Millennium, the Pope, the Roman Catholic Church, and so many other things. He is definitely the Blessed Mother's priest because he speaks in truth and light. I respect him greatly and know he is Our Blessed Mother's chosen "victim soul."

The book, "Finding God the Father," is a compilation of personal testimonies of parishioners that were given on a parish-wide weekend retreat. Monsignor Carroll speaks on numerous topics in the book. One topic that I have not heard before is in his own words.

He states, "I believe that Our Blessed Mother has been leading the Church, the faithful and the world to a reunion with God the Father. This is the final element of the Triumph of the Immaculate Heart of Mary, the crowning jewel of Mary's era of intercession, the presentation of God's children from the hands of their mother into the loving arms of God the Father."

As I contemplate the tremendous love and healing I have received, especially after my abortion experiences, I can only say, "Thank you God. I give love, praise, glory, and honor to You." People do not really understand the tremendous suffering and pain a woman and man endure from an abortion experience. I have had many people tell me how much they do understand, but they do not. It is only textbook understanding. I believe and will continue to say it over and over, unless you have had an abortion experience, you do not have the vaguest idea of what a woman or man endures.

The individuals that I truly believe understood to some capacity the suffering of abortion victims were the priests I was blessed with knowing personally and those I worked with. That is one reason I hold priests in such high regard. Their kindness and compassion while standing in truth and light is so comforting to me and those who were referred to them. In all the referrals I made to priests in the past ten years, I can honestly say, I have never had a woman or man come back to me with a complaint about a priest she/he was referred to from S.A.V.E. We were so blessed.

Upon completion of the S.A.V.E. program, I watched how God picked up the women and men literally from the pit of hell, transformed them into new life, and swept them into His loving arms with so much love that the women and men were overwhelmed. The S.A.V.E. Roman Catholic Healing Programs belong to God and He will raise them up so that His Will will be done. Many will try to imitate it, but they will fail.

I have come to Praise God for my trials and tribulations and sufferings and joys. Through the unspeakable love for God the Father, the devotion to the Passion and Death of Jesus Christ, the gifts of the Holy Spirit, the maternal love and patience of Our Blessed Mother, and being blessed with three dynamo Saints, St. Therese, St. Francis, and Padre Pio, I have learned that by suffering silently and asking for no consolation, it is a continuous prayer to God and it eases the continuous sufferings of Jesus Christ.

When I visualize one who suffers for God, I see a rosebud that opens up as the pain intensifies. The rose becomes the most beautiful flower with the most magnificent fragrance that rises up to heaven and to the Throne of God. This fragrance of suffering brings so much pleasure and joy to God, that He lovingly whispers in the sufferer's ear, "You are my beloved one, with whom I love to the depths of My Heart and with whom I show great favor." How awesome!

I pray that you will receive all the love and mercy that God desires for you. I pray that you say "YES" to God and do His Holy Will. I pray that you discern the call you have received from God by speaking to a priest or Spiritual Director. But most of all, I pray that you and your family will prepare for the Jubilee of the most magnificent event that this world will ever experience, the Triumph of the Immaculate Heart and the total and complete union of the Roman Catholic Church to the Holy Trinity.

This will only occur In His Truth and In His Light. Amen.
Alleluia. Praise God.

In His Truth and In His Light